PLATO'S ACADEMY
AND THE ETERNAL KEY

✳ ✳ ✳

ALI GRAY

Cover by Paul Roget

ISBN : 1495413500
ISBN 13: 9781495413506
Library of Congress Control Number: 2014903688
CreateSpace Independent Publishing Platform
North Charleston, South Carolina

To Rich, Lauren and Sophie

CONTENTS

1

THE LETTER

Charlie, when you read this letter, I will be dead.

Charlie had read the letter more than a hundred times but, even now, the hairs on his neck spiked upwards. He flicked the torch brighter under his bedcovers.

I know you will be sad for a while after I'm gone, but one day you will understand.

Charlie, I have written this letter to ask a favour of you. There is a scroll in the research room in the museum that is important. It is from Ancient Greece. But the scroll doesn't belong to the museum, it belongs in a special place and I didn't get a chance to return it. I need you to return it for me.

Go to the room (use your skill to get in). The scroll is on a shelf. Unlock the green panelled door behind the desk and go down the staircase, stay calm, and return the scroll. Thanks Charlie and good luck.

Your loving grandfather
Ted

From under the quilt, Charlie surfaced for air. He folded the letter into a tiny square and put it into his silver locket, the shape of a dice, dangling around his neck. The letter had played on his mind for weeks now — ever since Ted had given him the envelope in hospital.

'Don't tell anyone about this Charlie', Ted had said. 'This is between us.'

Charlie wanted to open the envelope right away. But Ted had insisted Charlie open it after he was gone. And out of respect for his grandfather, Charlie had waited. Now, Charlie regretted it. What was he thinking? His mind flipped over dozens of questions ... *Where does the scroll belong? ... What kind of a special place? ... Why do I need to stay calm?*

Taking a deep breath, Charlie switched off the torch. He lay on his back and gazed at the moonlight shimmering across his bedroom ceiling. He thought about Ted.

Was he really in a heaven — somewhere beautiful — somewhere perfect? Maybe he was watching over him right now. Maybe. His parents have faith. They go to church every Sunday. But why don't dead people give you a sign, a message, a signal, anything — letting you know they're okay. That's all Charlie needed.

Tucked under the covers, he rolled on his side. He stared at his acoustic guitar standing solitarily in the corner. He hadn't touched the instrument for a month now, not since Ted's death. Strumming guitar used to be a cheerful pastime, but lately there was nothing to be cheerful about. He doubted he would ever play music again. And he didn't care much if he didn't. Cold air drifted through the open window. He sniffed and swallowed hard.

His thoughts moved on to the next day's school excursion. Not allowed to travel into the city by himself, Charlie had waited weeks for this outing. He wished tomorrow would come sooner. He wished it was here now. Because tomorrow would be his only opportunity to do one final favour for Ted. Tomorrow he would be in the museum.

2

THE STAIRCASE

'Gather here, class, quietly please.'

Mr Hollingbury's eyes darted behind the thick glass of his spectacles. 'This incredible gallery is called the Parthenon Room — isn't it just marvellous?'

Like cows moving through stockyards, Charlie and his class inched through the gallery's entrance. Charlie stopped in the middle of the giant hall and eyeballed the marble blocks mounted along the walls. He didn't need any introduction to the Parthenon Room. He knew the room well. Ted had worked in the museum for over ten years. And, every second Sunday, Charlie and his mum would catch a train into the city and walk to the museum. There she would leave Charlie, while she went to her city office and caught up on paperwork. For the next couple of hours, Ted and Charlie would wander through the galleries together, just looking and thinking.

Glancing up at the massive skylight that somehow injected an unexpected liveliness into the sculptures, Charlie smiled. He remembered telling Ted that one day he would build a skylight just like it above his lounge room at home. Dark with a tiny window, his mum always complained about their lounge room. A big skylight would fix the problem.

'What a brilliant idea, Charlie', Ted had said. 'I'll help you install it.'

The thought of Ted balancing on ladder rungs installing a skylight warmed Charlie's heart. Bursting with enthusiasm, Ted always wanted to help Charlie. Always. But with Ted gone, someone else would have to help him now.

Charlie sucked in the cold breeze from the air conditioner and walked towards the white slabs running along the wall on the western side of the gallery. All were perfectly aligned and labelled with shiny brass plaques. At a waist-high rope, he stopped and thought about the task in hand — returning Ted's scroll. Nervously, he bit his lip. Today was the day. This was it. No backing out now. Charlie reached into his pocket for his wire to double check his trusty tool hadn't fallen out. The sharp piece of metal jabbed his finger. He took a deep breath and hoped he could remember everything his dad had taught him.

Mr Hollingbury shuffled in front of a group of headless statues at the rear of the gallery and loosened his tie.

'Can anyone tell me anything about the Parthenon?'

Peering over the black rim of his spectacles, the teacher waited for a response. He pressed his lips together. The class stood still, mute.

'Someone must know something about the Parthenon building.' His forehead creased. 'We studied all of this in history you know — we spent a whole session on it.'

Silence.

He shook his head and clicked his tongue. Then he looked at his watch.

'All right then — you have ten minutes to explore this room', he muttered. 'And we all know what tonight's homework is going to be.'

For the next ten minutes, Mr Hollingbury floated about the students like a bad smell, slinking from one side of the gallery to the other, asking more questions. Eventually, the teacher got tired of asking questions that no-one bothered to answer, and sat on a bench.

Like metal to a magnet, Charlie became drawn to a particular slab halfway along the wall. Etched into the block was his favourite scene — two fearless warriors on horseback. His heart fluttered when he saw the familiar men. The warriors reined back their horses, the animal's hoofs high in the air, in a blaze of movement. Charlie gripped the rope tightly, closed his eyes and blanked his mind. He remembered Ted's words.

'Feel the scenes Charlie — feel them', Ted used to say. 'If you shut your eyes and open your mind you can be there.'

If Charlie concentrated hard enough — he *could* be there. He imagined another world far away; a world of warriors and gods and horses and charioteers. He saw fire in the eyes of the brave men thrusting their swords like kings. Yells and battle cries penetrated his ears. Pumping veins bulged from the horses' necks and hoofs pounded the dirt. Then, he imagined Ted was alive and standing alongside him, right there in the gallery. He felt the warmth of Ted's hand and heard his breath. A weird kind of spirited energy burst inside him; the energy of the warriors. And, suddenly, Charlie had the courage of a lion. He opened his eyes and gazed at the horseman. Today he would need all the courage he could muster.

'All right everyone — next stop is the portrait gallery', barked Mr Hollingbury.

As the teacher gathered the class at the gallery's entrance, Charlie crept silently to the rear of the gallery. He slipped behind a statue and didn't move. He heard laughter and chatter soften. He didn't move. Footsteps faded into the whispers of the museum. He didn't move. Charlie waited and waited. When the room was silent, he looked out from behind the statue and Mr Hollingbury and his class were gone.

Charlie scuttled from large gallery to small gallery, display room to display room, one exhibit after the other, like a rat in a maze. Within minutes, he was standing outside a '*Staff only*' door. He kept glancing at his watch, pretending he was waiting for someone, but when nobody was about, he disappeared through the door and down several flights of concrete steps.

Alone, Charlie stood in the shadowy corridors of the basement. The air hung thicker in the basement, suffocating and badly ventilated. A musty odour filled Charlie's nostrils and his chest muscles tightened. Squinting through the haze, he worked out his direction, and hurried towards Ted's old research room. Over and over in his head, he repeated the room number: *216 … 216.* He tiptoed around a corner, eyeballing the digits on the doors as he went. There it was — research room 216. He checked either side of him, making sure no-one was coming and fumbled in his pocket for the wire.

Charlie's head pounded. His palms became clammy. He knelt down and pulled out his pocket torch and flashed it on the handle. Dust had gathered on the knob. He guessed no-one had been in the room since Ted had passed away. But Charlie couldn't be sure. What if someone was in there now? Gripping the torch between his teeth, he pointed the rays to the lock. With trembling fingers, he inserted the wire in the top part of the key hole and felt for the pins.

'A pin-and-tumbler lock', he whispered between the torch and gritted teeth.

Gently, he pressed the tip of the wire onto each pin. One by one, he pushed the pins upwards. He heard each one click as it set. On the last pin he heard a noise. *Footsteps.* He quickly set the pin. Someone was coming — around the corner. Too late to run, he applied pressure to the wire and turned the handle. *Click.* He shoved the door open and dived into the room. A light flashed at the other end of the corridor. Quickly, he switched off his torch and shut the door behind him. His chest thundered.

'Is anyone there?' shouted a security guard.

Charlie bit his lip. He pressed his back against the door and closed his eyes. He shouldn't be there. He was going to get caught.

'Anyone there?' yelled the guard again.

Charlie's whole body quivered. He dared not move a limb. Heavy boots thumped the concrete floor. He pressed his back harder against the door. The noise grew louder and louder. Then the footsteps stopped — right on the other side of the door. Charlie's heartbeat thumped into overdrive. His ears strained. Was he a goner? He held his breath.

To his relief, he heard the footsteps start up again, and slowly the noise faded down the corridor. He started breathing again.

Charlie waited for a long time in the darkness. When he thought it was safe, he switched his pocket torch back on. A thin ray of light flashed across the walls of the room and on to a shelf with a tanned leather pouch, the shape of a cylinder, sitting in the middle. He inched closer, hearing only the sound of his own heavy breathing. He could see the pouch had thick stitching down one side in funny shaped letters, probably Greek. Charlie hesitated. Frozen, he stared at the object lit up by the torch rays. He didn't want to touch it.

When Ted handled these old pouches he always wore special gloves. Charlie wondered if he should do the same. He shone the torch away from the pouch and around the shelves, looking for gloves.

He spied an old black and white photo on a shelf; Ted was sitting at the very desk in the room, smiling, as he worked away. This research room was Ted's special place. A quiet place to do the work he loved. And every time Ted took Charlie to the room, he would show Charlie a new scroll, from an ancient time, with a story behind it that Charlie had never heard before.

'These scrolls are much more than just stories written on old paper', Ted would say. 'We learn things from them Charlie — they teach us ideas.'

Then Ted would rub his ear. He always rubbed his ear when he made important statements to Charlie. Ted had a birthmark on one of his ears. But Charlie often wondered if it was really a birthmark at all? Charlie suspected it was from rubbing after all those important statements.

Ted was a genius, an expert curator, and could translate anything old. Anything. He was the best translator at the museum, the best in London. Early in his career, Ted had worked at the university, specialising in ancient languages. He became so good at translating handwritten scripts, the museum hired him full-time.

Charlie studied Ted's sparkling eyes in the photograph. He remembered the excitement in Ted's voice when he explained his latest project to him. But after a while, Ted sensed that Charlie was growing restless.

'Are you bored yet, Charlie?' Ted would ask.

Charlie wasn't bored, but Ted would pull an old box from under his desk anyway. Every time Charlie went to the museum, Ted had a new box, a new case, a new trunk, a new something. And the item was always locked. Charlie would grin like a bear at Ted, retrieve his wire from his back pocket and get to work on his latest challenge. For hours and hours Charlie worked.

When he was done, Ted would say, 'You have the gift of your father.'

Charlie's dad was a locksmith — and that was Charlie's skill — picking locks.

Without gloves, Charlie picked up the leather cylinder and untied the lid. He flashed the torch inside the container and saw a scroll tightly wrapped up inside. Charlie smiled as he re-tied the lid again. *Ted, I have your scroll*, he thought.

Tucking the cylinder under his armpit, Charlie pulled his wire from his back pocket, and flicked his school tie over one shoulder. He glanced at his watch — 11.15 a.m. Then he moved towards the green panelled door behind the desk.

Charlie couldn't remember seeing the green panelled door before. Perhaps he hadn't noticed it. A strange thought entered Charlie's head. Why did *he* have to return the scroll? Couldn't one of Ted's workmates from the museum have taken it back — someone with a key? He wiped his sweaty hands down his trousers. Biting his lip, he put the wire in the lock. But he couldn't feel any pins. He couldn't feel anything. The lock was like a black hole. Then something clicked. The door slowly opened.

Through the darkness, Charlie flashed the torch down a narrow corridor. Thin rays of light illuminated broken spider webs and the carcasses of dead beetles. Beyond the activities of the crawlers, he saw an outline of a staircase with steps going down. Two words from Ted's letter came into his head — *stay calm*. Why would Ted write that? The thought of staying calm made him nervous.

Charlie tightened his grip on the pouch and crept along the passageway, avoiding the lurking shadows. Slowly, he descended the staircase. Dark, rickety stairs creaked under his school shoes. From nowhere, an icy wind whipped his face. The torch blacked out. Darkness surrounded him. Then, he started falling. But he hadn't lost his footing. The staircase underneath him disappeared. Spiralling into a free fall, the torch dropped from his hand.

Helpless, Charlie's eyes darted around wildly. Wind ripped through his hair. He plunged like a rock in a pond. His stomach lifted to his throat. The skin on his cheeks stretched across his face and the saliva in his mouth dried up in an instant. He couldn't even scream. A horrible feeling came over him — he was hurtling towards his doom.

Then his body suddenly became lighter. The speed of the fall lost some of its intensity. His stomach dropped from his throat and sank back down under his rib cage. *Thump*. His body crashed to the floor. In the dark, he lay on his back. He pinched his arms and legs to check if he was alive. He felt the pinch. He must be alive.

3

THE DOOR

Straining his eyes, Charlie looked for outlines of things in the blackness. He hated being in darkness. Up until age six, he had slept with a tiny orange hall light on every night, anything to avoid those ghostly shadows. That tiny piece of electrical equipment had been his saviour. But that was years ago. He had long overcome his fear of the dark and didn't need that pesky orange bulb anymore. Or so he thought. He could use it now.

He touched the cold floor with his hands and felt his way up a rough uneven wall. He fingered his way across the wall, then he felt a smoother surface, like cold metal — a handle. He pressed down on it. *Clunk*. A door opened.

Light streamed into Charlie's eyes, momentarily blinding him. It took a second for his eyes to adjust.

Suddenly his clothes felt different — thicker and prickly. He glanced at his body and draped over one shoulder hung heavy linen. His school uniform had vanished. He almost stopped breathing. Where were his clothes? Even his shoes had disappeared. Instead, wide strapped sandals wrapped his naked feet. Quickly, he lifted the robe to his knees and became somewhat relieved when he saw his underpants. He reached for his silver locket; at least he still had that with Ted's letter inside. *Stay calm*, he said to himself. How could he stay calm? He wanted to scream.

Spying the pouch on the floor, Charlie bent over and picked it up. Terrified, he crept through the door. He found himself standing in a large room with leather cylinders and timber boxes stacked on funny shelves that looked like pigeon holes. An odd smell of leather and oak drifted up his nostrils. Suddenly it didn't feel like he was in the basement of the museum. It felt like he was somewhere else. He spun around in circles. *Where am I?* Nervously, he moved to a shelf and pulled out one of the cylinders. He untied the lid. A scroll was inside, just like the one tucked under his armpit. *What is this place?*

As Charlie returned the cylinder to the shelf, he noticed a statue of a lady with wings, in the corner of the room, near the door he'd come in. With her robe flowing to her ankles and her sword thrusting skyward, even she didn't look like she belonged in a museum basement. Charlie stared at the blank eyes of the stony faced lady and gulped.

'Can I help you good sir?' said a raspy voice.

Charlie jumped a foot in the air and dropped Ted's scroll. He scrambled to the floor and gathered it up.

A woman suddenly appeared from behind one of the shelves, her grey eyes sunken and her face drawn. She crept towards him, running her wiry fingers through thick grey hair. With thin and tired bones, her tunic hung from her body like a sack and one of her eyes didn't seem to move.

Startled by the odd-looking woman, Charlie froze.

'Am I able to help you good sir?' said the lady again.

'Err ... I want to return a scroll.'

'Certainly sir', she pursed her lips. 'You may place the scroll on the shelf.'

Charlie looked at the lady and then at the leather pouch in his hands.

'I ... I am not sure which shelf it goes on', he said.

'Then, can you tell me good sir, what is the title of the scroll in your hands?' Her voice was sharp.

With hands trembling, Charlie said, 'It's in an old language — I can't read it.'

He glanced at the stitching on the pouch as he spoke and saw writing he could now read.

'I *can* read it', he whispered, shocked. '*The Apology.*'

'Ah, *The Apology* ... *The Apology* goes on the shelf over there.' A bony finger with a dirty nail pointed to a shelf with a gap in it, along the back wall. One of her eyes moved in the direction of the shelf, the other stayed glued on Charlie.

Charlie darted towards the shelf. He repeated the words *stay calm, stay calm* over and over in his head. He slipped the scroll between two other leather pouches, all the time thinking about the writing he couldn't read before, but could read now. He turned to speak to the lady.

'See you later then', he said. His knees shook as he walked.

The lady stood still, with her arms crossed, watching him. She licked her thin lips. Charlie felt her moving eye on the back of his neck. He picked up the pace and dashed towards the door in the corner. He gripped the handle and twisted it.

'It's locked.' Charlie toyed with the handle. 'The door is locked. Why is it locked? I just came through it.'

The lady hobbled towards the door.

'That is most strange', she said.

'What?' snapped Charlie. 'What is most strange?'

He kept on flicking the handle.

'Well, good sir, usually there is a key in that door.'

The lady looked puzzled. She stooped over and her eyes scanned the marble tiles, as though she was looking for a key.

Charlie bent his head forward and peered into the key hole set in the heavy stone. The lock was the strangest lock he had ever seen. It didn't have the dual pieces of a pin and tumbler lock, or the single piece of a wafer. It wasn't a warded lock because it was without obstructions. What kind of lock was it? What kind of key was it? He scratched his head. Blood filtered up his neck and flushed his face. His heart pulsated. He knew he couldn't pick it.

'The key … where is the key?' Desperation crept into Charlie's voice. 'I need to go back up that staircase.'

'I hadn't noticed the key was missing — most strange', she said again.

'Is there another key somewhere?' Charlie asked.

He wanted to get out of that pigeon hole room. It was weird. He wanted to get away from the lady. She was weird too. He watched the lady's eyes glaze over as though she was thinking. She scratched her forehead with her grubby fingernail.

'Plato may be able to help', she said finally.

'Plato. Who is Plato?'

'Plato is our leader — he is the Principal of The Academy.'

She waved towards daylight streaming through a door on the far side of the room. One of her eyes blinked, and the other remained fixed on Charlie.

'The Academy', Charlie's heart thumped. 'What's The Academy?'

'You have not heard of The Academy, good sir?' She sounded surprised.

'No.'

'The Academy is a school — a school of great learning. You are standing in the library of The Academy.'

Charlie's jaw dropped. What was this odd-looking lady talking about? He stared at her as he thought about what he should do next. Her working eye stared back. He decided he had to leave her and find this Plato and get the key.

'What does your leader ... er ... Plato look like?' he asked.

'Plato is a tall man with broad shoulders; he is aged about thirty.' The lady smiled. 'You will know when you find him. He has eyes that look through you.'

Tentatively, Charlie smiled back.

'Er … thank you for your help — I'll go and find him.'

Charlie dashed towards the open door with the daylight streaming through, hoping it would lead him back to the museum basement, or at least somewhere that he recognised.

With her arms crossed, the lady watched Charlie leave.

Emerging from the library, Charlie stepped into the brightest of daylight, not the grey sky of London. The rays of the sun quickly heated his face. He found himself standing in the middle of a courtyard, next to a statue of a lion spurting water from its roaring jaws. He thought he was in a movie set. Odd-looking buildings with pillars surrounded him. People in strange tunics scurried past. But nobody blinked an eyelid at him. He looked for a film crew, or a movie star — neither to be seen.

Charlie's head pounded with questions. *What kind of a weird school is this? Why are all these people dressed in stupid clothes? Why am I dressed in stupid clothes?* Feeling sick, his eyes darted about the courtyard, panicked.

Then in the distance, over a set of rolling hills, Charlie saw a building on top of a rock peak, glistening like a block of gold — a picture of perfection. He recognised the structure at once — *the Parthenon*. But the Parthenon he knew was in ruins, crumbling and falling apart. No mistake — it *was* the Parthenon.

His mind raced. He rattled his brain for an explanation. If he wasn't on a movie set, he must be in the middle of an open-air exhibit at the museum — a realistic one.

Too realistic! A small boy dashed past. Charlie grabbed the lad's tunic from behind and reeled him in.

'What city am I in?' he asked.

'Athens', cried the boy. The lad tugged at his tunic and ran away.

Charlie's stomach churned. None of this made any sense. How could he be in Athens? He was in London fifteen minutes ago. More disturbing, how could he be in Athens at a time when the Parthenon was pristine? He looked at the gleaming structure on the hill again. Blood pumped to his face. There was no explanation. Now Charlie knew he was in trouble — real trouble. Somehow that staircase had led him here — led him to a different city and to a different time — an ancient time. And Ted had sent him — sent him to return a scroll.

4

THE LYRE

Charlie wandered around the courtyard, stunned and alone, trying to get his thoughts together. Old people and young, well groomed and scruffy, strong and frail, buzzed past Charlie in their funny robes. *If this place was meant to be a school*, Charlie thought, *why aren't these kids in class? And why were there so many parents and grandparents here? Maybe it was an open day.*

With marble buildings scattered around the court-yard, Charlie decided to enter one and take a look — try and find Plato. In one corner of a giant hall he saw children, aged about five or six, playing games with tiny wooden shovels and hammers. A lady played on the tiles with the young children. Other kids, about his age, gathered around the room in small groups. Some drew triangles and worked out angle calculations with white chalk on black tabletops. Others wrote fancy letters on scrolls. A number of kids just hovered around, talking and laughing. The school didn't seem to have many rules. Charlie liked the thought.

Charlie saw some older people sitting on a couch against the wall. A short stocky man stood in front of them and asked the group a bunch of strange questions.

'What is courage?' Charlie heard the man say.

'Courage is staying at your post, fighting your enemy and not running away', came one reply.

'What about men who fight in retreat? Are they not courageous? And what is courage in the face of illness?' went on the man, 'or courage in the face of wild winds at sea?'

The stocky man didn't let up. On and on he went. Charlie felt stressed just listening to the man rant. He backed away from the group and looked for a tall man about thirty. But no-one that age was in the hall. As he left, he wondered why some of the students were so old. Perhaps they had never graduated — they weren't smart enough.

Charlie walked into an enclosure, like a walled paddock, on the other side of the library. On the steps at the entry, he stood with a group of adults and watched the action in the field. He saw kids dressed in armour lifting strange weights. Boys fired arrows with crudely made bows. He saw one boy hurl a javelin. Or was it a spear? A group of girls wrestled each other on the grass. One of the girls, bigger and stronger than the others, took the smaller girls out — one by one. Fists flew and feet kicked. But each time the strong girl crushed her opponent. Her knees dug into her victim's stomach, she punched the air and her armbands flashed in the sun. Charlie felt uneasy watching the girl. He looked for a man fitting Plato's description but didn't see anyone. He quickly left.

Beyond the buildings dotted around the courtyard was a garden with little huts scattered here and there, and behind the garden was a high stone wall. Fenced in, Charlie's eyes followed the wall around the entire school, until he saw an open bronze gate. Happy the gate was open, at least he could escape.

Charlie walked towards the garden and stood under a fig tree, screening himself from the sun's burning rays. The earthy smells of the land filled his lungs. He touched his locket and thought about Ted's letter. *Stay calm,* he said to himself.

He saw a stone fountain amongst a cluster of olive trees. He inched towards it and drank from a spout. The water tasted clean and fresh — like the stream water where he camped with his dad. As Charlie slurped the water, he heard a strange strumming sound behind him. He tiptoed through the trees towards the music. Through a branch of olive twigs, Charlie saw a slight man with wide eyes, sitting on a bench strumming the strangest looking instrument.

Charlie's ears pricked up as he listened carefully to the chords. The music was unlike anything he had ever heard — kind of mystical. Then some kids, about Charlie's age, gathered around the man's ankles on the grass. They started to sing. Choir-like voices and soft notes filled the air. The rhythm of the instrument followed the words. He thought about his guitar at home — leaning against his bedroom wall. Something stirred in Charlie's heart. And for a brief moment, he forgot where he was.

Hidden behind a tree, Charlie watched the group for some time. He dare not move or attract attention to himself. After a while, the man on the bench stopped strumming. The kids stopped singing. Charlie heard the man send the group away. Then the man looked in Charlie's direction and waved him over.

'Come hither boy', said the man. His owl-like eyes sparkled in the sun.

Charlie stuck his head out from underneath a branch.

'I … I am looking for Plato', he said. He didn't want to get any closer.

'I am Glaucon, Plato's older brother.' Glaucon shuffled along the bench, and tapped the spot next to him, motioning for Charlie to sit down.

'And you are?'

'Charlie.'

For a second, Charlie hesitated. Should he go over to the man and sit down? He didn't have a choice. He had to talk to someone. How else was he going to find Plato? How else was he going to get the key and go home? He inched towards Glaucon and sat at the other end of the bench, leaving a comfortable space between the pair. He flattened his heels on the ground to stop his knees from quivering.

Charlie couldn't take his eyes off the instrument. It was made from a tortoise shell with two bow-shaped timber arms sticking outwards from the shell, almost like horns on a Viking's hat. At the end of the timber horns was a crossbar, with several strings stretching from the crossbar back to the shell. Charlie studied the shell's grey scales, the thickness of the strings, and the carvings in the horns – the object fascinated him.

'Have you not seen a lyre before, Charlie?' asked Glaucon.

'No', replied Charlie.

'Tell me, my friend, do you like music?'

'I used to …'

'I see.' Glaucon's eyes became sad. 'Something bad has happened and turned you away.'

Charlie felt uneasy.

'Would it please you to play it?'

'No!' said Charlie. 'I mean … no, thank you.'

Glaucon seemed surprised at Charlie's abruptness. He looked at Charlie's pale skin, his wide blue eyes, and his troubled look and said, 'Have I seen you before Charlie? Are you a student here?'

'No', said Charlie. 'Um … I came to return a scroll. I came down a staircase and through a door in the library — near the statue of a lady with wings. But now the door is locked and I can't get home. The lady in the library told me Plato might be able to help me', blurted Charlie.

'Ah … so you have had the pleasure of meeting Xenophon, our assistant librarian.'

'Yes.'

'The woman is a marvel; she treasures our wonderful scrolls and works tirelessly to protect them.'

Charlie tried to manage a smile.

'Tell me, Charlie, you speak in a strange tongue. Where are you from?' asked Glaucon.

'I am not from around here', replied Charlie. 'I … I just want to go home — I need to go back through the library door. I just need the key.'

'I sense your urgency, my friend', said Glaucon. He stared at Charlie and his face crumpled, like he was concerned.

'How old are you Charlie?' he asked suddenly.

'Eleven.'

Glaucon rubbed his finger over his bottom lip. His eyes glazed over as though his mind was a million miles away. A long awkward silence followed.

'My friend, if you have come through the door in the library, my brother will want to meet with you. This I cannot doubt.'

Tucking the lyre under his armpit, Glaucon stood up. Firmly, he placed his hand on Charlie's shoulder. Charlie felt his neck muscles tighten.

'You must follow me. I will take you to my brother.'

Charlie followed Glaucon back towards the courtyard. As they walked Charlie noticed that the sun was higher, and the rays were making weird patterns across the front of the marble buildings. Charlie guessed by now it must be early afternoon. But he didn't have his watch. He also noticed the activity in the school wasn't winding down. It was buzzing. More people than ever seemed to scuttle around him.

'What time does school finish?' asked Charlie.

'Ah … you propose a most interesting question, Charlie', said Glaucon.

Charlie didn't think the question was that interesting. He thought it was quite straightforward. He rephrased it, 'What time do the students leave?'

'Education is a lifetime, my friend. The Academy never closes ... and the students ... well they never really leave.'

Charlie gulped.

5

THE LIBRARIAN

Across from the library, Charlie followed Glaucon into a building with huge pillars at the front. He walked through a dining hall, with a long timber table in the middle. The longest table he had ever seen. Covering the table were bowls of oranges and apples, seeds of some type and mushy stews. Young children sat at benches along the table, playing games with round stones. Occasionally, they ate the food. In a kitchen, three men roasted small animals on a spit. Charlie couldn't recognise any of the animals. But they smelt good. Finally, Glaucon stopped at a door at the rear of the building and raised his knuckles to the timber, tapping gently.

'Plato, may I enter? I have someone you should meet.'

A faint mumble came from behind the timber.

Opening the door, Glaucon waved Charlie into the room.

Charlie walked across a large rectangular room, with a small glassless window that framed the courtyard outside. A tall, strong man, with massive shoulders, lay on the bed with his feet dangling over the end. As Charlie drew closer, he saw the man had his eyes closed, beads of sweat trickled down the sides of his pale face and his dark thick hair was tied back in a ponytail. The man had a fever. Memories of Ted lying helpless in a hospital bed flashed inside Charlie's head like a red warning signal.

'Plato', whispered Glaucon. 'I have brought someone special for you to meet.'

Lifting Plato's shoulders, Glaucon propped cushions behind his brother's back.

The eyelids of the man fluttered, he struggled to open them.

'Our guest is called Charlie. He came through the library door.'

Plato slowly opened his eyelids and took some time to focus. Charlie felt the intensity of his stare. It was as though Plato's dark eyes were looking for something inside him, inside his eyes — like his eyes were windows. He now knew what Xenophon had meant. That piercing stare forever etched into Charlie's memory. Plato raised his hand and signalled for Charlie to sit next to him on the bed. Inching towards the bed, Charlie sat down.

'Tell me, my friend', whispered Plato, his voice so faint Charlie had to move closer to hear him. 'How did you come to be in our library?'

Charlie fidgeted with his tunic and pulled the rope around his waist.

'Er ... I came to return a scroll — I put the scroll back on the shelf — but the door I came through is now locked. I need the key to get back.'

'I see.' Plato reached over a plate piled high with fruit and cake and grabbed a cup of water from his bedside table. The cup shook in his hands as he slowly sipped.

'And another question I must ask, where did you get this scroll?'

'Ted, my grandfather, asked me to return it.' Charlie scratched his head. 'I just need the key.'

'Ted.' Plato seemed surprised. His eyes widened and he glanced at Glaucon. The pair exchanged a look as if they knew something Charlie didn't. Carefully, Plato placed his cup back on the table.

'We haven't seen Ted for a month now', said Plato. 'How is our dear friend?'

Blood drained from Charlie's face. His cheeks turned whiter than flour. What was going on? Legs trembling, Charlie pressed his hands on his knees to stop them. How could these weird people know Ted?

'You knew Ted?' he said.

'Most certainly we know Ted', replied Plato. He coughed after he spoke.

Glaucon quickly dabbed Plato's forehead with a cloth.

'But I don't understand', said Charlie.

'Ted is our chief librarian', said Plato. 'He comes through the same library door you did.'

Plato's forehead crinkled. 'We miss Ted dearly.'

29

Charlie didn't know what to say next. How could Ted be a librarian in Ancient Greece? Ted was museum curator in the twenty-first century. Plato must be talking about someone else.

'I don't think we are talking about the same person', said Charlie.

At least he hoped not.

'Ted is a most unusual name', said Plato. 'It must be the same person.'

Charlie suddenly felt sick.

'What did Ted, um your librarian, look like?' asked Charlie.

'Ted's in his seventies. He has snow-white hair and — oh yes — he has a red birthmark on his right ear.'

Charlie's jaw dropped. He suddenly became winded — like someone had punched him in the chest. It *was* the same Ted. Ted *was* the librarian. Charlie was speechless; he didn't know what to say next. He went quiet for a moment. Then he whispered, 'Ted died.'

6

THE FRUIT AND
THE CAKE

Plato's chest wheezed. He struggled to draw air, like he was suffocating. Going into shock, Plato's eyes glazed over and filled with sadness. His pale lips pressed together and he stared at nothing for a long time. Glaucon didn't say anything either. He bowed his head and his eyes gazed at the tiles. He too seemed saddened by the news.

'I am sorry about the passing of your grandfather, Charlie', said Plato finally. 'Ted was a fine man, Charlie — a good man.'

Charlie nodded his head.

Plato seemed reflective.

'Ted's enthusiasm for us to record our work, record our ideas, was enduring', said Plato. 'Write your ideas down he would tell us.'

Plato looked at Charlie.

'You know, Charlie, your grandfather told us to write every day.'

Charlie wasn't surprised to hear this. Ted had told Charlie to do the same. Charlie remembered about a year ago, when he told Ted about a machine he was going to invent. A machine that could whip through oceans, thrash across land and glide through space. Ted had said, 'Write your ideas down Charlie — write them down.' Later that week, Ted had bought Charlie a notebook with a lock. Emily, his sister, was too young — she couldn't pick it and steal Charlie's ideas. So, in black pen, Charlie drew his machine in the book and put notes all over the pages as to how it was going to work. When Charlie showed the drawings to Ted he said, 'See, Charlie, ideas are ten times better when they are written down. They come to life. I love your machine.'

Tears started to roll down Charlie's cheeks. How he missed Ted. He wanted him back. But now he was crying in front of these strange people he didn't know. He wished he hadn't. With the back of his hand, he quickly wiped the drops away and hoped Plato or Glaucon hadn't noticed. But Plato did notice. He leaned across and grabbed Charlie's hand and held it. Charlie felt his weakness but also his warmth.

'Charlie, it is right that you shed tears for Ted. But you must remember what death is. Only the body dies in death, Charlie, not the soul. Ted's soul has now separated from his body and migrated to where it came from. This is a great thing, Charlie.'

'Migrated', sniffled Charlie. He could barely speak through his emotions.

'Yes, Charlie. Ted's soul has migrated, like a bird, back to the Eternal World.'

'What Eternal World?' asked Charlie. 'How do you know where Ted is?'

'Let me tell you something, Charlie, every one of us has a soul. Your soul is inside you — and Ted's soul was inside Ted.'

Plato leaned forward and pressed Charlie's chest with his fingers. A strange sensation moved through Charlie's veins, like a sedative was being pumped into his blood. He didn't know if he had imagined it. Then Plato reached towards the plate sitting on his bedside table. He grabbed a pear, an apple and a fig.

'My friend, hold out your hands', he said.

Charlie cupped his hands together and Plato placed the three pieces of fruit into his palms.

'Charlie our souls are divided into three parts. The pear is *reason*, the apple is *spirit*, and the fig is *appetite*.'

Plato touched the tops of the fruit as he spoke.

Charlie had never thought about having a soul before. If he did have a soul – he was sure it wouldn't look like fruit.

'The parts of the soul battle with one other.' Plato knocked the fruit about in Charlie's palms, as if the fruit were fighting with one another.

Charlie stared at the fruit being battered around. He didn't have a clue what Plato was doing or going on about.

'I can see you are confused, my friend', said Plato.

'Um … I'm not really following … why are you bashing the fruit? … And what is reason, spirit and appetite anyway?' asked Charlie.

Plato stopped knocking the fruit about and picked up a huge chunk of cake. 'Charlie have you ever tasted fruit cake?'

'Yes … but I didn't like it very much.'

'Well then, I want you to think of a cake you love, baked by someone you love', said Plato.

Charlie instantly thought of his mum's chocolate mud cake. With strawberry jam, cream and sprinkles, his mum made the best cake in the world.

'Are you thinking of the cake?' Plato put the cake back on the plate.

'Yes', said Charlie. 'My mum's chocolate mud cake.'

'Well Charlie, spirit is in your heart, you love that cake because it is baked by your mother. Spirit is your honour and loyalty to your mother shown through your desire for her cake. Appetite is in your stomach — it hungers for the cake. Appetite is impatient and tells your stomach it will starve without it. But Charlie, reason is the most important part; it is in your head. Reason tells you that too much cake will make your body sick. It says control yourself — only eat a small piece.'

Charlie thought about what Plato was saying. He could kind of relate to it. One time, at his own birthday party, he ate way too much mud cake — and he did get sick — so sick he vomited in the toilet.

Plato lifted his weak arms and untied the cord around his ponytail. 'And so Charlie, when *reason*, the pear, dominates the other parts ...' He wrapped the cord around the three pieces of fruit in Charlie's hands and tied a knot. 'Then the parts of the soul are working together; they become one, a soul in harmony.'

Plato smiled. 'The parts of Ted's soul were together Charlie, they were working as one. Ted's soul was in harmony.'

Gently, Plato put his hands on Charlie's hands and covered the fruit. Plato left his hands there for a long time. Charlie felt awkward. Part of him wanted to pull his hands away, but another part wanted to leave them.

'Ted was a good person, Charlie. This is why I know his soul has migrated to the Eternal World.'

Charlie looked at the red rings of sickness under Plato's eyes and the sweat seeping from his forehead. *Plato is dying*, he thought. But why was he thinking about Plato? Plato didn't matter to him. He was there to get a key — the key he needed to get home.

'The key to the door in the library', whispered Charlie. 'Plato, do you know where the key is?'

Desperation crept into Charlie's voice. Plato turned his head slowly towards Glaucon and his eyelids fluttered. Charlie sensed there was some kind of problem. Barely able to talk, Plato whispered, 'Charlie, we will do everything in our power to help you. The grandson of Ted is our friend.'

Charlie heaved a sigh of relief.

'But we do not know where the key is.' Plato closed his eyes and slowly opened them again. 'We noticed the key in the library was missing a month ago — about the time Ted left. We were waiting for Ted to return — we thought he might know where the key is.'

'Is there a spare key?' Charlie asked.

'There is only one key.'

Charlie's heart pounded.

'The Oracle', said Glaucon.

Plato looked at Glaucon and nodded.

'There is one person in Greece who will know where the key is.' Plato's voice faded as though he was losing strength. 'The Oracle.'

'The Oracle', repeated Charlie.

Glaucon picked up the cup for Plato and held it to his brother's lips. Trickles of liquid spilled from the sides of Plato's mouth, down his chin.

'Where is the Oracle?' asked Charlie.

'The Oracle resides in a Temple at Delphi', said Plato. 'Charlie, to find the key you must seek an audience with the Oracle. She will know where the key is. You must tell her I am your friend. And you will need someone from The Academy to accompany you on your journey to Delphi. Indeed you will need help.'

'I shall make the journey', said Glaucon. He put the cup back on the table.

'No, I think not', Plato spluttered and shook his head. 'This will not do. My dear brother, you are needed here in The Academy. You are a captain and must steer the ship. Your importance here cannot be misjudged. And it is certain I am getting weaker by the day.'

'Charlie, we will send you on your journey with our brightest student.'

Plato waved his hand. 'Adonia will accompany Charlie to Delphi.'

Glaucon nodded at his brother.

Plato leaned forward and gripped Charlie's arm. 'I fear, Charlie, your journey will be dangerous, but take with you the light of your mind — it is the light of the truth.'

Charlie looked at the gaunt face of Plato and saw a fiery passion in his eyes. But what was Plato talking about? Why would the journey be dangerous? And what light in your mind? Plato's words didn't make any sense. But, for some reason, Charlie nodded his head in agreement. He wasn't sure why.

Plato slumped back into his blankets and closed his eyes. Charlie hoped that he hadn't died. He was relieved when he saw Plato's chest rise and fall.

'Come Charlie', Glaucon signalled. 'We must find Adonia and get your supplies.'

7

THE STRONG GIRL

Charlie sat quietly on the marble steps leading to the library. He gazed across the courtyard, past the lion fountain, and watched Glaucon disappear into a mud hut on the edge of The Academy. While he waited, Charlie rummaged through his sack of supplies, scrounged together by Glaucon in the kitchen. Squashed in the bag were a small clay urn, freshly baked bread, apples and pears, and seeds Charlie had never seen before. He assumed the seeds were to be eaten, not planted. The urn weighed down the sack and Charlie wished he had a plastic water bottle.

As Charlie sat quietly, pondering his predicament, his head rattled with questions. He thought about Ted visiting Ancient Greece every day to work in the library. It would explain the scrolls Ted used to show Charlie. But the key must have been in the door when Ted came to the library, otherwise Ted couldn't have got back. But what happened to the key? And why does the Oracle know where it is? What even is an Oracle?

Charlie's mind raced until Glaucon emerged from a hut with a tall girl. Her long brown hair swept from side to side as she walked towards him. A sack dangled from one of her hands. As she drew closer, Charlie realised it was the strong girl who had wrestled the other girls earlier. He stared at the muscles in her toned upper arms, protruding through elaborate armbands of snakes. Her white tunic, gathered around her waist with a rope belt, hung above the knees of her powerful legs. Close up, she looked like a female version of the warriors etched onto the slabs in the museum. She stopped in front of Charlie and stared at him. The sunlight radiated her face. Charlie hesitated for a second, then smiled. But she didn't smile back. Charlie guessed she was about his age.

'My name is Adonia', said the girl. 'I am your companion to Delphi.'

'Hi there', said Charlie.

Adonia turned towards Glaucon and spoke as if Charlie wasn't standing there.

'He speaks a strange language.'

'Very true. He visits us from afar', replied Glaucon. 'He is the grandson of Ted, our old librarian. Did you ever come by Ted, Adonia? Did you ever meet Ted in the library?'

'No. I have little time for reading', she said.

Charlie started to worry about Plato's choice of his companion. She was meant to be his best student, but she didn't read much. Something didn't ring true.

Raising her hand, Adonia squinted into the sun.

'We must start our journey now', she said.

'How far is Delphi?' asked Charlie.

Adonia threw her sack over her shoulder.

'Two sunrises by foot.'

Charlie eyeballed his flat leather sandals. He wished he had his Nike runners. He had never walked for two days straight. Had he ever walked for two hours straight? If he had, he couldn't remember it.

Glaucon placed his hand on Charlie's shoulder and squeezed it, as if he was trying to reassure him. His owl-like eyes gazed at Charlie; they seemed darker, full of fear. Charlie felt the seriousness of his stare. Taking a long time to speak, Glaucon chose his words carefully.

'My friend, perhaps when you return you will do me a great honour, you will play the lyre', he said.

Glaucon's eyes surged with tears. Charlie didn't know if the tears were for him or for his dying brother, Plato. Either way, death hovered on the horizon.

But what if Charlie did die on his journey to Delphi — nobody would know. In his mind, he saw his mum and dad at a news conference, barely speaking through their tears. Even Emily, his sister, was crying. He imagined them holding up pictures of Charlie, a missing person, with a phone number to ring. Then, after the police had lost interest, his mum and dad would spend the rest of their lives looking for him — in supermarkets — in shopping centres — in the hope they would find him again. But they never would ... a pointless search. Their lives wasted.

And if he did die out there — he wouldn't get a proper funeral; he would just rot in the sand. No family. No friends. Nothing. A lump got stuck in his throat. Why didn't he tell someone about Ted's letter?

'Come', said Adonia, 'We must leave.'

She started hiking. Charlie chased after her.

'The speed of the gods!' yelled Glaucon.

8

THE YELLOW EYES

Adonia led Charlie along a dirt trail into the foothills. They passed white farmhouses with red-tiled roofs and tiered terraces dotted with olive and lemon trees. But as they trekked higher the trail became more rugged and harder to see. Thick grasses and bushes smothered the track. Eventually, they couldn't see a track at all, as if the undergrowth had swallowed it. And the number of farmhouses dwindled and then disappeared altogether. As they climbed higher, Charlie's puffing turned into panting and then his panting turned into wheezing.

By mid-afternoon the sun's blazing rays had roasted Charlie's fair skin to a pink crisp. Charlie tried to cover his face with his hands, but the heat and the glare were relentless. He wished he had his block-out cream. But he hadn't. Not wanting to say anything to Adonia, he pressed on. But after another hour, he had to say something.

'My skin is burning Adonia — from the sun', he said.

She stopped, looked at his skin and, without saying a word, started hiking again. Charlie scuttled after her and wished he hadn't said anything. They trekked on for another hour without talking. But the silence was killing Charlie. He couldn't stand it any longer.

'Adonia, what exactly is the Oracle?' he puffed.

She kept on walking, whipping the grass with her stick.

'Come on. We're going to be stuck together for a few days — you might as well talk to me.'

Silence.

'Tell me about the Oracle. *Please.*'

Adonia stopped walking, turned to face Charlie, broke her stick over her knee and picked up a bigger one.

'You have no knowledge, great or small, of the Oracle?'

'None.'

'Everyone knows of the Oracle.'

'Not me.'

'She is a priestess. She lives in the Temple of Apollo.'

'Is she some kind of god?'

'She speaks for the god Apollo. She has divine powers. People seek her counsel.'

'Ask her questions you mean?'

'Yes. Her answers are always true.' Adonia paused for a second. 'But then, sometimes, her answers can have different meanings.'

'Have you met her before?'

'No. We have never met', she said.

Adonia appeared bored with Charlie's questions. She started hiking again. They bulldozed their way through bushes so thick that Charlie nearly got wedged between them. Adonia charged her way through the shrubs like a wild boar, leading Charlie deeper and deeper into the undergrowth. Charlie looked for a long stick. He found a thick one like Adonia's and started whipping the grass like her.

'I met with Plato at The Academy', he said.

'Plato is not long for this world — he is dying', said Adonia.

Charlie knew this already. He saw the fever in Plato's eyes; the same fever that captured Ted.

'Is Plato a teacher at The Academy?' he asked.

'You ask a lot of questions', she said, frowning.

'Just interested', said Charlie.

'Plato started The Academy. He is the founder, a teacher, mathematician, astronomer and philosopher.'

'Plato is all those things', said Charlie. 'Impressive.'

Charlie thought about Plato as he hiked. He wondered how he could be an astronomer without having a telescope. He didn't know much about Ancient Greece, but he knew they didn't have telescopes. Studying the stars without magnification — how hard would that be? Then he thought about Plato being a philosopher. He knew what a philosopher was — Ted had told him. They were people with ideas. Big ideas — about the world and about people. *No wonder Ted wanted Plato to write his ideas down*, thought Charlie.

Adonia climbed over a large rock on the lip of a mountain. She stood still, on the edge of a cliff, like one of the statues in the museum. She viewed the valley beyond and frowned, as though she was angry with it.

Charlie watched her. 'You don't want to be here, do you?'

'No', she snapped.

A hot wind picked up and battered Charlie about his ears.

'Look, I'm sorry', he said. 'But I really need to get that key — it's really important to me — I need it to get home.'

'You have interrupted my training', she snarled.

Adonia bent down and picked up some dirt, like an animal tracker.

'You are training for something?' asked Charlie.

'To be a warrior.' Dirt sifted through her fingers.

'Awesome', said Charlie.

She gave Charlie another icy stare and tossed the dirt to the ground.

'We stay here for the night', she said.

Under the white light of a full moon, Adonia gathered small branches and dry leaves and bunched them together in a heap. She pulled a stone and an odd-looking stick from her sack and lit a fire. Her dark pupils enlarged as she stoked the blaze. Thin wisps of smoke and tiny specks of ash drifted up Charlie's nostrils. An urn appeared in Adonia's hands, and she bit the cork out with her teeth and spat it on the ground. She passed it to Charlie.

'Drink', she said.

Gripping both clay handles, Charlie peered through the neck and gagged at the sight of the lumpy white liquid.

'What is it?' he asked.

'Goat's milk.'

Charlie stomach growled. He had never tried goat's milk before. He would prefer not to drink anything at all, but he didn't want to appear rude. Well, not as rude as Adonia. Slowly, he sipped the milk and, to his surprise, it was thick and flavoursome. He quite liked it. He guzzled some more. A film of white lined his upper lip. He grabbed some bread and crunched into it, nearly breaking a tooth. Adonia watched him grapple with the rock-hard crust.

'You are not from around here?' she said.

'Is it that obvious?' Charlie chewed the bread like a horse.

Adonia threw rocks at the fire and watched Charlie gnaw. She didn't ask Charlie any questions — which Charlie thought was strange. But she didn't care about Charlie or the key. After a while, Adonia's relentless stare unsettled Charlie. He stopped eating and sat quietly, staring into the twisted flames.

He remembered his dad's bonfires in his backyard at home, much bigger than this one. Every Saturday, Charlie liked to help his dad with the garden. Together, they raked up leaves into small piles scattered across the yard like oversized ant hills. It was important that they put the leaves into piles and waited for the leaves to dry out, otherwise they wouldn't burn properly. When the leaves were dry, he and his dad would move the piles into a giant heap in the back corner of the garden and set fire to it. And when Ted came to stay with them, before he went into hospital, he would sit on the back porch with a rug on his knees and watch them stoke the blaze. Some of the time he watched but most of the time he was asleep.

But then, when Ted went into hospital — he never came out again. Charlie looked away from the flames and up to the stars, the tiny spectacles of light. He waited for a sign from Ted. He searched for patterns in the galaxies, a secret message, letting him know that Ted was all right. But like the stars outside his bedroom window, the heavenly bodies didn't have a message. They had nothing for him. They ignored him. Tightly, he clung to his locket.

'Did you hear something?' said Adonia suddenly.

'I don't think …'

'Shoosh!' she snapped.

Charlie's eyes scanned the shadows of the night. The crackles in the trees suddenly became louder. Blood pumped to his throat. He sat frozen. With his ears strained, every snapping twig and every rustling leaf became a predator, ready to strike.

Adonia jumped to her feet. Charlie did the same.

Leaves rustling and branches snapping came from a few yards behind them — near the rockface. Charlie heard a snarling sound. Adonia crept towards the cliff's edge. She pulled a knife, tucked under her belt, and slowly peered over the edge. Charlie inched behind her and looked over the edge to the darkness below.

A blur of white fur shot out from the darkness and pounced over their heads. Adonia slipped and fell over the cliff. Charlie lunged at her. He caught her wrist. Her body weight slammed him to the ground. She dangled at the end of his arm, swinging like a pendulum.

'Hold on', screamed Charlie. 'Hold on.'

Charlie lay on his stomach. Adonia's weight was pushing him towards the edge. There was nothing to hold on to. He needed an anchor. Her screams bounced off the rocks around them. Two yellow eyes flashed in front of Charlie's face. The creature hissed. Then the eyes vanished.

'I'm slipping!' yelled Adonia.

Charlie gritted his teeth and tried to pull her up. But he couldn't lift her. He slid closer to the edge. He was losing his grip. Then Charlie saw moonlight flash on Adonia's knife. He stretched across the dirt and snatched it. He stabbed it into the ground. Using the knife as an anchor, he roared like a bear and heaved Adonia up.

Back on flat ground, Adonia panted like a dog. Lying in the dirt, she looked to the stars.

'Thank you', she whispered. 'You saved my life.'

Charlie didn't speak. He couldn't. Black diamond pupils set in yellow eyes kept flashing in his head.

9

THE ORACLE

Charlie and Adonia rose with the sun. Neither of them had slept a wink. Too many unidentified barks, howls and shrieks made for a nervous night. Charlie wanted to skip breakfast and get moving. But Adonia insisted they eat to maintain strength.

'You have to stay strong, Charlie', she said, 'your body and your mind.'

She passed some bread to Charlie.

'This time pour milk on the bread', she said. 'It softens it.'

Charlie looked at Adonia and wondered why she was telling him this now. She could have told him that yesterday. He shrugged his shoulders and soaked the bread in the milk. As he bit into it, he realised that this technique worked well and he wondered why he hadn't thought of it. Adonia smiled at Charlie as she watched him eat. Then, after breakfast, she stamped out the smouldering coals with her open sandals.

'We should get moving', she said. 'We have a key to find.'

They packed their sacks and left the campsite quickly.

At the next flowing stream Adonia submerged her ankles in the lapping waters. With a stick, she mixed fine sand with water. Charlie wondered what she was doing — perhaps doodling in the mud. He rested on the grass on a nearby bank and watched her slop up the sandy water in her cupped hands, careful not to spill any.

'Come hither Charlie', she shouted from the stream. 'Come.'

Charlie bounced off the grass and went over to her.

'My friend, stretch out your arms', she said.

Standing opposite her, Charlie raised his arms. His muscles tensed as he did. She slopped the muddy concoction all over his arms and legs. The mud was cold and stuck to his skin like glue easing the sunburn in seconds. She finished the routine by putting streaks of grime across his cheeks.

'That will protect you', she said.

Charlie touched the fine sand on his face. 'You know, you don't have to be nice to me — just because of last night.'

'You saved my life.'

'Anybody would have done the same.'

'No. I owe you.'

In truth, Charlie didn't mind this new friendlier Adonia. It was better than the girl he was stuck with yesterday. But it felt fake. Really fake. He was just about to say something when a strange look came across Adonia's face. Her eyes met with Charlie's but she wasn't looking at him. She was looking through him. Charlie suddenly felt awkward.

'Are you all right?' he asked.

She didn't say anything at first. Then she blinked and her mind seemed to be back with him.

'That sand on your face', she whispered. 'Reminds me of my father.'

'Your father', he said.

'Yes. My father was a great warrior. He fought battles in the fields over there.'

She pointed over Charlie's shoulder, to the grasslands behind him, on the flat of the valley.

Charlie turned and stared at the fields. The long grass swayed back and forth in a light breeze. He wondered if Adonia's father was still alive, but he didn't like to ask her. Her face looked sad as she stared at the fields, motion-less. She appeared lost in her thoughts.

After a long time she said, 'My father died in the war.'

'I am sorry, Adonia', said Charlie.

She kept on staring at the grasslands. Then she smiled as though she had accepted her dad's passing.

Charlie watched her long hair blow in the breeze. She looked so alone. Then he stared at the grasslands and started to think about the warriors on the slabs in the museum. Those brave men on horseback he had spent hours studying with Ted. *One of those men could have been Adonia's father*, he thought. *Who knows?* Then, Charlie heard Ted's voice in his head, 'You can be there

Charlie — close your eyes and open your mind — you can be there.' And sure enough he could be there — because he was. And he didn't have to close his eyes; he had to open them.

Looking down the valley, across the grasslands, to the summits in the distance, Charlie thought about the warriors, the horses and the battles. But he was in his own battle – a battle to return to his normal life. He needed a key. He sucked in the morning air and turned to face Adonia. Her eyes moved away from the grasslands and directly towards Charlie. For a second, they stared at each other, not saying a word. But Charlie took comfort in her sad eyes; they understood each other.

'Come', she said. 'We have many hours ahead of us.'

The pair started hiking again.

✳ ✳ ✳

On the second day of their journey, Adonia and Charlie arrived in Delphi early afternoon. They stood on a large limestone block, in the top row of a semi-circle amphitheatre, and observed the bustling chaos below. Villagers dressed in festive clothes lined the streets in some kind of weird procession. Carrying baby goats, lambs and live chickens, baskets of oranges, figs, eggs and olives, they laughed and danced in the street.

'A day of offering', said Adonia. 'To the gods.'

Charlie watched the parade move towards a black marble altar. On the platform, tubby men in long robes read from scrolls and accepted the gifts, which then disappeared through a doorway behind the altar. Not to be seen again. The villagers scurried away, happy but empty-handed.

'What do those men do with the animals and the food?' asked Charlie.

'They are priests. They deliver the offerings to the gods', replied Adonia.

Sure they do, thought Charlie, looking at their beach ball stomachs. *They eat it all themselves.*

'There it is.' Adonia pointed to a building. 'The Temple of Apollo.'

An enormous building, larger and whiter than the others, stood pride of place in the centre of the bedlam. A red and blue frieze wrapped the building under a red tiled roof, and sunlight bounced across the fluted columns at the front. Charlie's muscles tensed in his neck. He knew the Oracle was his only chance of getting home.

'Come on!' Adonia charged down the oversized steps.

Charlie dashed after her. Once on flat ground the pair ran up a ramp. They hid their sacks behind a large clay urn and crept between two giant shiny doors and entered the Temple. A large toothless man with a face covered in brown stains and open sores greeted them from the shadows. Not fazed by the man's grotesque appearance, Adonia shook his hand. She whispered in his ear and slipped him a coin. *Why is Adonia paying him?* thought Charlie. *The man hasn't done anything.* Then the man muttered something incoherent, which Adonia seemed to understand.

As the man mumbled, Charlie noticed his tongue had been sliced clean off. What happened to his tongue? Could it have been lost in a war? Charlie imagined that. Never again could the man speak of his hard-fought battles, his scars or his wins over weaker men. All of his great fights would remain stories untold. Charlie heaved a sigh for the man, but kept his distance. He didn't want to catch anything. He followed him into a giant hall. Then the man disappeared just as he had entered, into the dark shadows of the pillars.

Inside, Charlie eyeballed a strange room, with strange wall art; fanged pythons at war with red-eyed dragons. Charlie made a beeline for a couch against a wall and slumped in between the silk cushions. He rubbed his heels. The thick straps on his sandals had sliced his skin into ribbons.

In silence, Charlie and Adonia waited, studying the unsettling frescos on the walls. Nervously, Charlie fidgeted with the rope at his waist. The building gave him the creeps.

Then, an icy wind whipped Charlie across the face, whisking his hair and flapping his tunic. Hairs on his neck stood upright. His lips quivered.

'Speak!' boomed a voice from above.

Charlie looked up. At the rear of the temple, on an embankment of steps, stood a lady with long black hair and matching black eyes — so black, Charlie couldn't see her irises. Her creepy black eyes were set against the purest white complexion. Draped across her slender body was a long black gown, with gold inlays that sparkled like tiny fairy lights. She patted a strange white cat in her arms as the huge rings on her fingers flashed.

Adonia stood up and bowed in the direction of the woman. Charlie didn't budge.

'We have come to ask you a question', said Adonia.

'Ah', she said. 'A question.'

She looked at the cat. 'Spiros, these people have come to ask us a question. That is what people do, Spiros. They ask a lot of questions.'

The cat purred.

The woman, who Charlie assumed was the Oracle, descended the stairs like a queen. She bent over at the foot of the staircase and gently placed the creature on the tiles. It howled in delight and bolted towards Charlie.

As the creature raced towards him, Charlie realised the animal was not an ordinary cat — it was a white lion cub. The cub hissed and scratched his ankles. But then Charlie saw the animal's eyes. He had seen those pupils before. *Black diamonds.* It was the animal from the night before — the very creature that nearly sent Adonia to her death. The cat snarled. Sharp pointed teeth opened and revealed a slimy pink tongue. Not thinking, Charlie pushed the cat away with his hands. But the cub swiped at him with a claw and gouged his finger.

'Ouch!' Charlie jumped to his feet. 'Your lion bit me!'

'Spiros — don't bite our guests. Not yet anyway.'

Charlie put his finger in his mouth and sucked the blood.

'Your cat was in the mountains last night – it nearly killed us!' He shook out the pain in his finger. 'You knew we were coming here.'

Adonia sneered at the animal that had toppled her over the cliff. The Oracle looked at the cub and grinned — as though she was proud of it.

'The Oracle and Spiros see everything', she said. 'People see nothing.'

Charlie glared at the Oracle.

'Where is the key that belongs in The Academy's library?' he blurted.

The Oracle's black eyes pierced Charlie's. She looked furious. Charlie knew he had done something wrong. She zoomed towards him, her gown sweeping the tiles. Between two black painted nails she seized Charlie's locket and, with his chain, pulled his face to hers.

'That is not how you address the Oracle', she snarled.

Charlie snatched the locket from her fingers and tucked it back under his tunic.

Her black eyes dilated in rage.

'The key from The Academy', snapped the Oracle. 'That key belongs to Plato. Why should I tell you where the key is? I tell only Plato.'

She spat on Charlie as she snarled and delivered him a cold angry stare. Then, she stormed towards the Temple's giant doors, her cape gliding across the tiles as she moved. She stopped at the doors and pointed to them. 'Leave my presence at once.'

Spiros raced over to his master and circled her.

'We are friends of Plato', shouted Adonia. 'He has sent us to you. Plato was too ill to travel with us.'

'Excuses … excuses. People give me nothing but excuses. It tires me.'

She pointed at the door again. 'Get out!'

The lion cub hissed and growled.

'We are not going until you have told us where the key is!' Charlie flung his arms in the air. 'I can't get home without it.'

The desperation in his voice ricocheted off the marble walls. The Oracle seemed surprised by the sudden outburst. She stood as still as a statue. Her eyes joined his. After a few seconds, she smiled wryly and crept back over towards him. Her black eyes fixed on his as she moved. If there ever was a time when Charlie felt intimidated, now was it. He bit his tongue and dared not speak. The Oracle stopped and turned her head towards the cat. She tapped her knees.

'Spiros — to your mother.'

The lion cub leapt into her arms. She stepped forward and held the animal in Charlie's face. The creature snarled through its fangs.

'Tell me boy — you do not belong here, do you?'

Charlie didn't answer.

'I know why you are here', she whispered through clenched teeth.

After a few long seconds, she turned her back on Charlie, and walked away, cuddling the cat. 'If you are who you say you are, truly friends of Plato, then you must know Plato's ideas. On this I will test you — three times.'

'Three times', repeated Adonia.

'I like to be sure.' The Oracle turned and smiled. 'If you succeed — you will have the location of the key.'

'And if we fail?' asked Charlie.

'Well then, my boy.' She stroked the cat. 'You will have gained nothing, you will not return home, and our paths will not cross again. Ever!'

Charlie swallowed.

The Oracle crept towards the couch. Her voice softened.

'Please', she waved to her guests. 'Sit down.'

Adonia and Charlie both moved to the couch and sat down.

The Oracle sneered and waved her rings. In a split second, the couch collapsed and Adonia and Charlie fell through a trap door. They screamed as they dropped.

10

THE CAVE

Adonia and Charlie fell into a black pit, their bodies twisting and tangling. Blood rushed to Charlie's head. His heartbeat skipped into overdrive.

'Are you all right Charlie?' whispered Adonia.

'No.' His voice echoed around the pit. He clambered to his feet.

'The Oracle did not like us', said Adonia.

'And I didn't like her', snapped Charlie. 'Or that nasty lion of hers.'

'There is a tunnel down here — this way', whispered Adonia. 'Stick close by.'

Charlie wasn't going to do anything else. He gripped Adonia's tunic at the back and inched along behind her as an icy chill raced down his spine. A strange smell of stuffiness, like damp earth, filled his lungs. Water splashed onto his ankles, soaking his sandals and making his legs itch.

'I see a light ahead', said Adonia.

Suddenly, a gust of wind whipped their necks.

'What's happening?' yelled Charlie.

'Aaargh!' screamed Adonia.

Something clamped around Charlie's throat — something as heavy as lead. The pressure nearly strangled him. He felt the same weighty force on his legs. The heaviness drove him to the ground.

'I can't move Adonia!'

'Nor I!'

'Oracle', shouted Charlie. 'Why are you doing this to us?'

No reply.

Sweat dripped from Charlie's forehead into his eyes. His vision blurred.

'I think we have chains on, Charlie — the Oracle has chained us.' Adonia spoke through gritted teeth. 'I can't even turn my head.'

Charlie sat on his backside. He tugged at the metal digging into his skin. A heavy neck brace wrapped his throat, making it difficult to breathe. Then he pulled at the tackle clamping his legs. He couldn't move.

'Why?' screamed Charlie.

Silence.

'Look, Charlie, on the rock face', said Adonia.

Charlie's eyes could barely focus. He peered through the murky haze at the strange shadowy images on the rock wall in front of him. Images of different vessels — bowls, pots and urns – drifted along the rock. Then he saw weirder, sinister images, like shadows of statues of people, pigs, horses and dogs. They passed across the rock face like a puppet show. The odd images were illuminated by a flickering light which seemed to be coming from behind him — perhaps a fire.

Charlie's brain rattled as he tried to comprehend the situation. The Oracle had chained their necks and legs. He touched his locket. *Stay calm.* He tried to pace out his breathing. He needed to think straight. But then he heard voices alongside him. Other people were down there with them. He heard their moans and the rattle of chains.

'There are other prisoners', said Adonia. 'Down here with us.'

'I know — I can hear them.'

'I will speak to them.'

Adonia shouted to the captives, 'How long have you been here?'

'All our lives', replied one of the prisoners.

'That's not good', whispered Charlie.

'No', said Adonia.

'Do you know where we are?' yelled Adonia.

'With you ...' replied the prisoner.

What kind of a stupid answer is that? thought Charlie. But when he thought about it some more — it made sense the prisoner had no idea where he was. He had been chained in one place all his life. How could he know? Charlie heard drops of water. Peering past his chained feet, Charlie saw water splash onto a pointed rock, the shape of a finger — a stalagmite.

'Adonia, I think we're in a cave', he said.

She didn't reply.

'I think we're in a cave', said Charlie again. He waited for a response. He knew she was there. He could hear her panting.

'I heard you the first time', she whispered. 'Charlie, this is not good.'

'No kidding!'

'No, I mean — I think I know what this is.'

Charlie tried to turn his head to face her. But the metal gripped his neck like claws. The slightest movement caused the metal to slice painfully into his skin.

'What is it?' he cried.

'We are prisoners in a cave — it must be the Oracle's first test.'

11

THE PRISONERS

'Charlie', said Adonia. 'Can you hear people talking behind us?'

Charlie pricked up his ears. He could hear voices alongside him — the other prisoners — but he wasn't sure about voices behind him. He looked at the shadows — for all he knew the voices could be coming from them.

'I am not sure what I hear', he whispered.

'There are people behind us', said Adonia.

'People. What people?'

'There are people behind us — carrying pots and statues — casting those shadows. I know what this is, Charlie. We are in a story that Plato tells. The Oracle is testing us.'

'We are in a story', gasped Charlie. He tried to turn his head. 'What story? What's happening?'

'Plato tells us a story about prisoners trapped in a cave. The prisoners have been in the cave all their lives, chained at the neck and legs.'

Charlie's heart raced.

'All that the prisoners can see are the shadows on the walls — the shadows we see now.'

Charlie stared at the images on the rock face and swallowed hard.

'The prisoners think those shadows are real things. But they aren't. They are just shadows. There is a low wall behind us, and a camp fire behind that. People are walking behind the wall carrying pots, statues and animals, made of wood and stone, on their heads. We can't see the people — we can only see the shadows of the things they are carrying.'

'What happens in the story?' barked Charlie. 'How does it end?'

He wasn't sure he wanted to hear the answer.

'A prisoner breaks his chains, sees that the shadows aren't real, and escapes the cave to a real world — the world outside.'

'So we need to escape – and get outside?'

'Yes. I think this is right. And maybe the Oracle will tell us where the key is.'

Charlie tugged at his neck brace. He couldn't stand the metal choking his throat for another second. The shackle around his neck must have a lock, even if it was from Ancient Greece. Locks hadn't changed much over the centuries. If he found a hole, a bolt, a peg in the brace, he knew he could open it. He ran his fingers slowly around the rim of the metal and felt a tiny metal peg on the side of the apparatus.

Adonia heard Charlie moving his chains.

'What are you doing?'

'I found a peg', said Charlie, '… in the brace.'

He needed to push it through the hole with something equally thin. He looked at his strappy leather sandals — useless. He touched his locket and chain — worse. He wished he had his piece of wire. Then he remembered Adonia's armband with the snakes. The jewellery was finely crafted and he wondered if Adonia could twist one of the snakes off.

'Adonia, your armband … do you think you could pull off a snake?'

'You will offend the god Medusa', she said.

Charlie didn't care who he offended.

'Could you at least try?'

Charlie heard her chains move. She raised a hand to her armband and slid the bronze craftwork off her arm. Her chains rattled as she tampered with it. A twisted snake appeared between her fingers in front of his eyes. He grabbed it.

'Thanks', he said.

The thin piece of metal sizzled in Charlie's hand. He felt for the peg with the end of the snake. His fingers sweated as he fiddled.

'A tough one …'

Charlie's fingers jiggled as his chains jangled. He carefully pushed the peg.

'Got it!'

Adonia grinned at Charlie. 'You too are impressive.'

In a flash Charlie's neck brace was off.

'Take that!'

He slammed the metal against the rock. It nearly bounced back and hit him in the face. He rubbed the red marks scored into his neck. Hunched over, he found the hole in the metal brace around his legs, and unlocked it. He quickly moved over to Adonia and released her from the shackles.

'Free of the chains', she squealed. 'Quick — look for a way out.'

'But what about the others – those poor guys?' said Charlie. 'We can't leave them here.'

Charlie could now see their young faces and shivering bodies. They were boys, the same age as him.

'Leave them — they know nothing else.'

'But it doesn't seem right.'

'Leave them', said Adonia again. 'Our task is to pass the test – and find your key.'

Charlie frowned at Adonia. He didn't agree. But there was no time to argue with her. He left the boys there, cold and chained up. But it felt all wrong.

12

THE SUN

Like disorientated squirrels, the pair crept along the edge of the cave, trying not to splash in the puddles. They inched towards a low wall, running across the middle of the cave, and hid at the back of a moss-covered rock. Behind the wall, Charlie could see people in robes walking along a path. They carried statues and pots that cast the shadows on the rock in front of the prisoners. And beyond the people on the path, he saw a huge camp fire burning at the rear of the cave.

Charlie watched the strange people carry their wares. Then, on the other side of the cave, he spied a hole with daylight coming through.

'Look Adonia', Charlie pointed. 'Daylight.'

'We will have to go across the top of the wall', she said.

'We can't', whispered Charlie. 'Those people carrying the stuff will see us.'

'No — they are lower', said Adonia. 'It is our only way out.'

'But the prisoners — they will see our shadows', snapped Charlie, not convinced by the plan at all.

'Make your body look like a pot — or an animal — and try not to scare them.'

Adonia darted out from behind the rock and climbed on top of the wall. She turned her body side on and Charlie could see her shadow on the rock face, right in front of the prisoners. With one hand, she fanned her fingers over her head and, with the other, she splayed it from her backside, making a five fingered tail.

Charlie stared at her shadow. If she was meant to be an animal, it wasn't a creature he had seen before — or ever wanted to see.

'I am a rooster', she whispered. 'Quick, follow me.'

Fearless, she inched along the top of the wall in between a pig and a dog.

With his whole body trembling, Charlie climbed the wall. He stood face on to the rock and placed his hands on his hips, dipped his head and bloated his stomach.

Adonia glanced at the shadows. 'You make a great urn, Charlie.'

Behind Adonia, Charlie shuffled along the wall on the balls of his feet, careful not to make his sandals squeak. The pot bearers below his ankles didn't notice him. They didn't even look up. They talked as they carted their pots and statues, like they were doing deliveries.

When Adonia and Charlie reached the other side, they jumped down from the wall and scurried towards a narrow hole in the rock, just wide enough to burrow through. Squeezing their bodies through the opening, they dragged their bruised and battered legs, chasing the trickles of light. At the top, sunlight blazed into the cave's opening.

Dazzled by the sun, Charlie quickly raised his palm to his eyes to block the glare. At first, he couldn't see anything, but as his eyes adjusted he could see rocks, trees, water, and finally he could see the sun.

Not recognising anything, his heart sank like a stone. He slumped onto a fallen tree branch and rubbed his swollen legs. The Oracle wasn't to be seen either, or her nasty little pet. He felt good about that.

'Where are we?' he said.

Adonia didn't answer. She waited for her eyes to adjust. When she saw the strange land she looked confused. She placed her hands on her hips and stared at the sun. Her face became intense.

'We must have done something wrong', she said.

She sat next to Charlie.

'Tell me Plato's story', said Charlie.

'Plato speaks of prisoners that are trapped in a cave; they see only the shadows on the wall. They cannot turn their heads and see the real objects. Then a prisoner breaks his chains and escapes the cave, through a narrow hole. The prisoner arrives outside, into the real world, and is at first dazzled by the light. But in time he sees the sun.'

She faced Charlie. Their eyes interlocked.

'We are the prisoners who escaped the cave. We see the sun.'

Charlie looked at the sun. 'Then what happens?'

She frowned and thought hard, squinting at the giant ball of yellow.

'The prisoner with the highest knowledge of all sees the sun', she said.

Charlie didn't interrupt.

'Plato says the prisoner who sees the sun — has to go back down into the cave — and tell the others there is a world outside.'

Her brown eyes glazed over, but then she smiled.

'The sun — that is it!' Her face beamed. 'It is a story with a message!'

'A message? What message? I don't understand!' barked Charlie.

'The prisoner who sees the sun sees the Eternal World.'

'The Eternal World', said Charlie. 'What's the Eternal World got to do with anything?'

Adonia wasn't making any sense. Charlie was lost. He didn't know what she was talking about.

'Plato's cave story is about a person seeing the Eternal World.'

The excitement rang through Adonia's voice.

'But we can't see the Eternal World.' Charlie flew his hand in the air and pointed. 'We can only see the sun.'

'Don't use your eyes', said Adonia. 'Use the light of your mind.'

Then Charlie remembered what Plato had said to him. Use the light of your mind, he had said, it is the light of the truth. What is the light of your mind? He wondered — or the light of the truth? He stared at the sun, hoping to see the Eternal World. But he didn't see it. He saw a blazing yellow ball, the cause of his sunburn.

Adonia jumped to her feet.

'We have to go back in the cave', she said. 'We have to free the prisoners.'

'You've changed your tune', said Charlie. 'You wanted to leave them five minutes ago.'

'I was wrong', said Adonia. 'We lead them to the sun; lead them to the Eternal World. It is the Oracle's test.'

Charlie shook his head. Never had he been so confused. But deep inside, he wanted to go back down and free the prisoners. If he didn't, guilt would plague him — for the rest of his life.

13

THE FIRE

Adonia disappeared down the rock face like a girl on a mission. Her voice echoed from the black hollow. 'Bring the snake!'

Charlie scurried after her, back into the shadows of obscurity.

Together, they slid down the slippery limestone and skidded across the slimy mould. Every footstep and every whisper reverberated around the cavity's walls, like the murmurs of ghosts. On tiptoes, they crept back along the low wall, in their rooster and urn disguises. The people at their ankles, carrying the statues, continued their deliveries, totally unaware of them. Like sewer mice in a drain, they scurried towards the prisoners.

Charlie knelt down in front of one of the prisoners, a young boy with a dirty face, and stared into his terrified dark eyes. He sensed the lad's fear. He recognised it. The same fear stung him on the inside, like a parasite. With trembling hands, he pulled out the snake tucked behind his ear.

'It's all right', he said. 'You'll be free soon.'

'Who are you?' screamed the boy. 'Why are you here?'

He struggled in his chains, trying to back away from Charlie.

'We are here to help you', said Charlie. He pushed the snake in the boy's neck brace and the peg fell. The brace opened.

One by one, Charlie released the prisoners — the chains at their throats first, then their legs. Initially, the boys didn't stand up. They didn't move. They seemed scared. Why didn't they jump for joy? Did they want to be set free? Charlie couldn't understand it.

After some time, the prisoners slowly clambered to their feet. Charlie watched them as they struggled to stand. Then, they stretched out their arms, like birds spanning their wings, ready to take flight. Nervously, the captives turned their heads away from the shadows and looked at the camp fire behind them. But the fire was too bright; they squinted, winced in pain and held their eyes, and then quickly turned their heads away.

'Leave us be', cried the boy with the dirty face. He moaned and touched his eyes.

'They don't seem that happy', whispered Charlie.

'They look angry', replied Adonia.

She waved to the boys.

'Come hither! Come over here.'

She tried to lead the boys over to the low wall.

'You see', she pointed to the wooden objects. 'They are real – not the shadows.'

The prisoners didn't care about the objects casting the shadows. They kept squinting and touching their eyelids. They became more agitated by the minute.

'I think the fire is too bright for them', said Charlie. 'They prefer to look at shadows.'

Then the boy with the dirty face stood on a rock, like he was the leader of the group. 'You are here to harm us!'

'No!' shouted Charlie. 'We won't hurt you!'

The boy snarled and whispered something to the other prisoners. He glared at Charlie. 'You are here to kill us!'

'No. You have it all wrong!'

The boys all started yelling at once, waving their fists. Then they charged at Adonia and Charlie, like bulls stampeding. One of the boys hurled his chains. The metal whizzed past Charlie's ear.

Charlie's eyes popped out from his head. 'They're trying to kill us!'

'Run!' screamed Adonia.

Adonia scampered up a rock face and Charlie sprinted after her. She tried to reach the hole leading to daylight, but had to quickly change her course. Two boys cut her escape route off.

'Quick, Adonia, this way', yelled Charlie.

Footsteps pounded the rocks behind him. Snarls and roars filled his eardrums. His heartbeat raced. Charlie sprinted towards the low wall and climbed up it as quickly as he could. Adonia scampered after him. The pot bearers stopped, and saw Charlie and Adonia scuttle across the wall. They froze like the statues they carried. Charlie jumped from the wall and landed on the path. Adonia landed behind him, knocking a pot bearer flying. A ceramic pig smashed into a thousand pieces.

'Towards the fire!' pointed Adonia. 'There's a tunnel behind it.'

Charlie and Adonia charged towards the fire. Giant flames scorched their skin as they dashed past. Their sweat splashed onto rocks beneath them. Footsteps pounded behind. They darted down a narrow tunnel, lit by burning torches jutting out from the walls. Sucking in oil fumes, they ran and they ran. Eventually, the footsteps faded. The tunnel went quiet.

'I think we have lost them', panted Adonia.

Then suddenly, the Oracle appeared from the haze in the tunnel with a restless cat in her arms.

14

THE IDEAL CITY

'You returned to the cave', boomed the Oracle. 'You tried to lead the prisoners to the sun — to the truth — to the Eternal World.'

Her black painted nails stroked the cub's fur and the flames from the torches on the walls reflected in her rings.

'You are not as stupid as you look.'

Under heavy makeup, her black eyes glared at Charlie.

'And Spiros, we did think they were stupid, did we not?'

The cub licked its lips and exposed its grotesque tongue.

Charlie stared at the cat and hoped the Oracle wouldn't let the creature loose in the tunnel. Sensing Charlie's fear, the cub half smiled. The Oracle glided closer to Charlie, her black gown swishing as she moved. With wiry fingers, she picked up Charlie's silver locket.

'But, of course, some humans can't see the Eternal World', she sneered in Charlie's face. 'That is Plato's point — is it not Spiros?' She cuddled the cat and the animal purred.

'Some humans don't want to see the Eternal World. Instead, they kill anyone who attempts to lead them to it.'

Charlie felt the venom of her stare. He dare not speak.

She let go of his locket and turned away.

'You have passed the first test — Plato would be impressed.' She twisted one of the rings on her fingers. 'If, of course, he was here and – I am sorry to say — he is not.'

A cynical smile stretched across her face.

'We have proved we are friends of Plato', said Adonia. 'We know his story of the cave — tell us where the key is.'

'My dear girl, you have passed the first test only', she snarled. 'I do not expect to see you again after the second.'

Her thundering laugh bounced off the tunnel's walls. A shrilling roar came from the cub. The earth started to shake and Charlie's legs wobbled with the vibrations. He stared at the ground rattling under his feet. He almost lost his footing. When he looked up again, the Oracle and the cub had vanished.

Adonia and Charlie edged deeper into the tunnel. Ahead, they could see a faint glow, streaming down the murky burrow, not far ahead. When they reached the light, the tunnel suddenly terminated. They entered a large square room, with high, uneven, blocked walls. Not a door or a window in sight. A giant granite table sat in the middle of the room with a dozen terracotta oil lamps burning feverishly around the edges. On the table was a miniature city with strange little figurines and tiny plaques with delicate inscriptions. Charlie stared at the two-inch high ceramic people and caught his breath.

Whoosh. In a flash, a giant limestone wall slid across the room's entrance, sealing off the tunnel, and leaving Charlie and Adonia entombed in the room.

'She's trapped us again!' barked Adonia.

'The cow!' shouted Charlie.

No reply.

Charlie peered over the painted ceramic figurines on the table and looked at Adonia. A small orange flame burned from the nozzle of one of the terracotta oil lamps and strangely illuminated his face. He picked up one of the little painted men and studied it under a flame.

'What do you think this is?' he said.

Adonia didn't answer. She moved to the limestone walls and pressed the blocks with her palms. 'This place looks like a dungeon.'

'You're freaking me out', said Charlie, in a high-pitched voice.

'Shoosh', said Adonia. 'What is that noise?'

Charlie pricked up his ears. 'A grinding sound — like heavy stone being dragged across the floor.'

'Charlie, the walls!'

'What about them?'

'The two walls either side of the table are moving — moving inwards!'

Charlie's eyes became fixated on the wall opposite him. His heart raced. Was this the end? He was going to die down here, in a dungeon. Crushed to death by moving walls ... and not a soul in the world would know.

Adonia moved quickly away from the walls and towards the table. Her eyes were glued on the tiny figurines. She plucked up one of the ceramics and examined it.

Charlie watched her as she shuffled thoughts inside her head.

'It is a king!' she said finally. 'It is a *Philosopher King*.'

'Is that good?' asked Charlie.

'Yes, Charlie. I think it is. The Oracle has given us a puzzle for the second test. I think we have to create Plato's ideal city.'

'Plato has an ideal city?' asked Charlie.

'Yes. He has ideas on how a city should work: who should be in charge, who does what job, how people should be ordered. The Oracle is testing us on Plato's city.' Adonia's eyes sparkled. 'We match people with their jobs and lay out the rules. It has to be it.'

She studied the table intensely. 'This second test will be a test of my memory.'

Charlie eyeballed the moving walls. The giant blocks were only four feet away from the table's edge and grinding inwards. He glared at Adonia. He knew his options were limited; rely on Adonia's memory or be crushed to death. He felt like an ant in the shadow of a boot.

'Philosophers are the rulers of Plato's ideal city', said Adonia. 'He calls them the *Philosopher Kings.*'

She pointed to a group of figurines with crowns, holding scrolls, and then she pointed to a cluster of tiny thrones.

'Put the Philosopher Kings on the thrones.'

Charlie didn't think it was the best time to question Adonia about Plato's ideas. But he couldn't help himself.

'Philosophers as leaders of the city — that doesn't sound ideal', said Charlie. 'Sounds self-serving and corrupt. What if other people want to lead? Why not vote people in?'

'No. Charlie this will not do. You speak of democracy. Plato says it doesn't work. Democracy does much harm. People don't vote for the good of the city, they vote for themselves — their own political interests.'

'But democracy is fairer, everyone has a say. We have democracy where I come from — it is the only way', said Charlie.

'Does it work?' asked Adonia. 'Are people not after power and their own self-fulfilment?'

Charlie had to think about this.

'Sort of works', he said. 'I think ...'

'Well, Plato thinks philosophers are best equipped to run the city; they are wise and govern with reason. They seek not power, but the good of all. Moral leaders if you like.'

Charlie placed a handful of Philosopher Kings on the thrones. He had to trust her. Then he lifted a handful of painted warriors, gripping swords and shields, wearing strange helmets.

'Here's a bunch of warriors, where do they go?'

'*Warriors* are a second class of people — they go right there.' Adonia pointed.

In trembling hands, Charlie placed the warriors in front of the miniature city walls.

'Warriors protect the city from enemies. They are strong and spirited', she said. 'Men of great courage — like my father.'

Adonia's eyes glazed over. Charlie was sure she was thinking about her dad. Tears welled in her eyes, and she sniffed. Under her breath she whispered, 'Send me your courage, Father.'

Charlie wished he had some of her dad's courage as well. Any courage would do. He glared at the walls and his head throbbed. He focused back on the table. With his fingers trembling, he lifted a handful of little men, some clutching shovels, others gripping hammers.

'What about these guys?' Charlie's voice wavered. 'Where shall I put them?'

Adonia's eyes came out of their mist and she focused again.

'They are the third class — the *Workers*. The farmers, potters and carpenters; they produce food, make pots, build houses and furniture. They desire things, have appetite. Put them in the workshops and on the farms.'

'So, Plato splits the city into three classes …' said Charlie.

'Yes', said Adonia. 'It is the best way for the city to function.'

'Classes of people — sounds backward.'

'Classes are good, Charlie — people know their job — people know their place.'

Adonia continued to study the table.

Charlie picked up a handful of little plaques, with thin strings attached, on the tips of his fingers. He read the inscription on one of the tiny signs.

'This sign says *Allowed to lie.*'

Adonia looked at the figurines. She seemed confused. Her finger pressed against her lip. Charlie glanced at the walls shifting inwards again and wished she would hurry up.

'We haven't got much time left, Adonia.'

'I cannot remember which class Plato says is allowed to lie.'

'You have to remember. Quickly, Adonia!'

She picked up a farmer. Charlie passed her a plaque. She held her breath and hung the sign around the farmer's neck. *Whoosh.* The walls accelerated, tripling their pace. Charlie flung his arms at the walls. His eyes popped out. He choked as he shouted.

'Take the plaque off, Adonia — it's not right!'

Adonia ripped the plaque off the farmer's head. She tossed the little worker against the wall. The ceramic smashed into smithereens. The walls slowed down, back to the regular speed.

'Not the workers', she said.

'Who is it then?' Charlie had to remember to breathe.

'Maybe the Philosopher Kings', she said. 'Maybe they can lie.'

'Are you sure?' said Charlie. She didn't look sure. 'I thought Plato talked about truth.'

'Yes. I remember now. Plato says the Philosopher Kings can lie to the other classes. It keeps the city in order.'

'That can't be right. Leaders shouldn't lie to their people', protested Charlie.

'It is for the good of the city.'

The walls progressed forward. Charlie's heart thrashed. The plaque had to go somewhere.

'On a King then', he said. With hands shaking Charlie hung the plaque around a Philosopher King's neck. He glared at the walls. The walls moved inwards at the regular pace. He blew air in relief.

'You were right, Adonia.'

She smiled.

Charlie grabbed another little sign and held it up on his fingernail.

'Responsible for education.'

'Put that sign around a Philosopher King's neck', said Adonia. 'Plato says philosophers should decide on the education of the classes.'

'Two more plaques — both say *No possessions.'*

'Yes. Yes. Give one to a warrior and one to a Philosopher King', said Adonia. 'Plato says the philosophers and the warriors need nothing. The workers provide food, goods and shelter for the others.'

'What about these women?' said Charlie. 'Where do they go?'

'Plato says women are equal to men', said Adonia. 'Equally as useful — they can be in any class.'

Charlie scattered the women randomly over the miniature city.

The giant block walls were now only two feet away from the table's edge and inching forward every second. The stench from the oil lamps burned Charlie's nostrils. With the back of his clammy hands, he wiped sweat from his roasting face. He struggled to breathe.

'Get up on the table, Charlie', ordered Adonia. 'Our time left is short!'

15

THE BALANCED SOUL

The pair sprang like leopards onto the marble table top. Charlie's legs shook in time with the vibrating walls. The limestone blocks scraped inwards. Charlie glared at the walls, which started to chip away the table edge. A small piece of marble shot upwards and hit Charlie above the eye.

'There is nothing left to place!' Adonia glared at the blocks. 'Why will the walls not stop?'

She clenched her teeth as she tried to push back the walls. She pressed with all her might. Her arm muscles swelled – she was going into the fight of her life.

Charlie flung his back against one of the walls and pushed.

'Where is Plato's ideal city?' he barked.

'It doesn't exist', said Adonia through clenched teeth. 'It is just Plato's idea.'

A shower of small stones smacked Charlie in the face.

'That's why we can't stop the walls', shrieked Charlie. 'The city doesn't exist!'

Dust blustered about the room, sending Charlie into a coughing fit. The walls continued to demolish the edges of the table, catapulting the figurines out of the miniature city, banishing them forever into exile. The rim of the heavy table top crumbled into fine powder. Charlie stretched out his arms and pressed his hands against the coarse blocks, trying with all his force to push back the walls. But the walls advanced like a road truck. Nothing would stop them. They were both going to die.

'We can't hold these walls!' Charlie's feet skidded on the table top.

'I do not understand', cried Adonia. 'This is Plato's ideal city. The Philosopher Kings represent reason. The warriors represent spirit. The workers represent appetite. They work together in harmony.'

Charlie's eyes widened.

'What did you say?'

'They work together in harmony.'

'No — before that — about what they represent.'

'Reason, spirit, appetite — working together.'

A light bulb flashed in Charlie's head. He remembered Plato with the fruit, the parts of the soul — the pear, the apple and the fig — reason, spirit and appetite. He remembered Plato knocking the fruit in his hands.

But when the three parts of the soul are bound together they become one — a soul in harmony.

'Adonia — I think this table is about the soul.'

Adonia winced as the veins in her neck swelled under her skin. 'It is what?'

Sweat dripped from Charlie's face. 'I think we need to tie the three classes together.'

One of the terracotta oil lamps slid across the table and spilled hot oil across the crumbling model city. The lamp smashed to the ground.

'By Zeus — you could be right. Quick, we have little time.'

Charlie dived across the table. Oil splashed on his hands. He grabbed a *Worker* and a *King*.

'Get me a *Warrior*', he shouted.

Adonia lunged for one of the warriors. The walls hammered more stone from the table. She tossed the warrior to Charlie. He crouched down on the table, now the width of a doormat. With swollen hands, he untied the rope at his waist and wrapped it furiously around the little men.

The walls stopped dead.

Silence struck the room. Charlie and Adonia crouched together, cramped and immobile, covered in a thick layer of dust. They could barely breathe. Only one terracotta oil lamp remained, and the flame danced, as if it was the only flame left in the universe.

Charlie wiped dirt from his face. 'I thought we were goners.'

'As did I.'

Charlie should have felt relieved. But he didn't. He just felt sick — sick to the core. The walls slid slowly backwards, away from the table. And a staircase appeared.

The Oracle swept down the steps.

16

THE MIND

'The balanced soul', said the Oracle. The cub trailed behind her.

'Reason, spirit and appetite — working together in harmony. You have surprised us, have they not Spiros? You know Plato's classes in his city represent the parts of the soul.'

Her black eyes flashed at Charlie. The cub flashed its fangs.

'I am enthralled by your knowledge.' Her sarcasm rang about the room.

Slowly, the Oracle crept towards Charlie. The cub followed. She leaned into Charlie's face.

'I know what you need.'

'I just need the key', said Charlie. 'Please tell us where it is. Then we'll go.'

'Ah ... the key. But this is not about a key is it?'

The Oracle ogled Charlie's locket.

Charlie quickly tucked the silver box under his tunic.

'Open it!' she yelled. The cub hissed.

Charlie didn't move.

Adonia bit her lip as she watched Charlie defy the Oracle.

'Open it now or I will rip it from your neck and feed it to Spiros.'

The cat swiped at Charlie's ankles and clawed red marks into his skin. Charlie tried to kick the creature away, but he couldn't. The cat swiped again.

Adonia touched Charlie's shoulder. 'Charlie, open it.'

Reluctantly, Charlie reached for his locket. He clicked it open and pulled out the note. Before he could speak, the Oracle had snatched the piece of paper from him. She unfolded the letter slowly with her black fingernails, her rings sparkling. Charlie watched her dark eyes roll across the page. After she had finished reading, she folded the letter and gave it back to Charlie. He quickly put it away.

'This person called Ted. Where is he now?' she snarled.

Charlie didn't answer her; he held his head in his hands.

'Where is he?'

'Tell her what you know', insisted Adonia.

'He is dead!' shouted Charlie.

The Oracle looked into the depths of Charlie's eyes and smiled at him. 'This is the reason you are here.'

She turned and slipped away into the haziness of the tunnel. 'Your final test will be in the Temple of Athena.'

When the Oracle and the cat had gone, Charlie and Adonia jumped from the table top, ran to the staircase, and climbed towards daylight. Outside, they found themselves in the shadows of the Temple of Apollo. The procession was over. Villagers were leaving the site with empty baskets and carts. Only a handful of roaming chickens and stray dogs remained. The smells had changed too. Putrid odours hung in the air; animal dung and rotten fruit, made worse by the afternoon heat of the sun. Charlie pegged his nose and avoided the strays. They went to find their sacks.

Adonia and Charlie made their way towards the Temple's porch. They saw the clay urn under the walkway but their sacks, tucked behind, had vanished. They combed the outskirts of the temple looking for their belongings. Then, the toothless man came from the shadows. His strong arms clutched their bags at the top. Adonia grinned at the tramp. He muttered a few unintelligible words that caused Adonia to open her sack. She pulled out the urn, unplugged the cork, and saw the man had refilled the vessel with milk.

She slipped him another coin. For a second there, Charlie thought the man's eyes had gone watery, his emotions not far from the surface of his unfortunate skin. His pus-filled scabs appeared redder and more inflamed in the sunlight. But Adonia ignored his sores and gently touched the man's face. She gave him the warmest of smiles. *In her own way,* thought Charlie, *she does care about other people.* He should do the same.

Charlie put out his hand. The man's eyes widened, as though he wasn't expecting it. He shook Charlie's hand and smiled. Charlie's heart lifted and he felt good inside.

'Come, Charlie.' Adonia raced up the amphitheatre steps.

'Where to now?'

'Athens', she replied. 'The Temple of Athena.'

Charlie looked down at the deep cuts in his feet, the blisters on his heels and the bruises on his legs. He rubbed the scores from the chains around his neck. His whole body ached. He didn't know if he could walk another two days back to Athens. He watched Adonia sprint up the steps. He wondered if she ever felt pain. She didn't show it if she did. But that's what warrior girls do, he supposed. Show no pain. Otherwise she wouldn't be a warrior. Then he noticed the toothless man waving at Adonia and, for some reason, the pain lessened. He climbed the steps.

✳ ✳ ✳

After trekking for hours and hours, darkness rolled across the skies. Too exhausted to eat, they drank milk from the urns, lit another fire and lay down in the dirt. With their blankets pulled to their necks, they lay like two parcels delivered to the night.

As Charlie lay, he heard owls hooting from the branches overhanging and occasionally he saw their eyes. He watched different black things crawl across the folds of his blanket. Some creatures were long and thin, some short and round, some fast, some slow. He pulled the blanket higher.

'Are you asleep Adonia?' he whispered.

'No.'

'Can I ask you something personal?'

'Of course.'

'Do you think there is a life after death?'

'You speak of the sun outside the cave. You speak of a soul in harmony migrating to such a place. You speak of the Eternal World.'

'Yes … I suppose I do.'

'Yes, of course, there is such a life — an immortal life. We learn about the Eternal World at The Academy.'

'What do you learn?'

'Plato teaches us there is a world, not like this one. A world where everything is permanent, timeless, nothing changes — a perfect world, Charlie.'

Charlie heard her exhale.

'One day my soul will be in such a world. I will be reunited with the souls of my dear parents.'

'Your mother is dead as well?' asked Charlie. He was shocked. He couldn't imagine a life without his parents.

'Yes. Both my parents are gone.' Adonia sighed heavily.

'That's terrible — I am sorry.'

'Do not concern yourself with me. I live well. Plato took me into The Academy after their passing. Now my duty is to Plato. And I do not look to the past; I look only to the future. And it is no concern to me, whether my future is short or long.'

'So you don't care if your life is short?'

'When the body dies, Charlie, the soul lives. If I die tomorrow I will be happy — happy in the Eternal World with my parents.'

Charlie watched another black dot crawl across his blanket.

Adonia leaned across him and flicked it off.

'One thing The Academy teaches you is that bad things can happen in this world. But you must maintain a soul in harmony, be a good person on the inside.' She clenched her fist and tapped her chest.

Charlie sucked in the chilly night air.

'Why do you ask about the Eternal World?' said Adonia

'My grandfather, Ted, the librarian in The Academy, died recently', said Charlie.

He pulled the woollen blanket to his chin.

'He believed in the Eternal World. He believed in a life after death. Before he died he believed he was going to heaven and I shouldn't worry about him. But the truth is that I worry about Ted every day. I worry about where he is. I can't do anything else but worry', he said.

'Why do you bother your mind with worry, Charlie?'

'If he was really in another world — The Eternal World — the least he could do is send me a message. Tell me he's fine. But he doesn't, Adonia. He doesn't send me anything.'

A lump got stuck in Charlie's throat.

'Charlie, it is not possible to rely on your senses to receive such a message from the Eternal World. Messages from the Eternal World can only be seen with your mind.'

Adonia raised her hand, her armband reflected in the moonlight. She touched her forehead.

'Only your mind', she repeated.

17

THE TEMPLE OF ATHENA

Late in the afternoon, Adonia and Charlie walked through the city gates of Athens. They hurried along narrow winding streets towards the market square.

In the square, Charlie elbowed his way through the chaos, trying not to lose Adonia. Market growers shoved lemons and figs in his face, fishmongers brushed his legs with baskets full of sardines and tuna, winemakers rolled barrels at his feet. All the while seagulls circled above. Dodging the madness, Charlie followed Adonia up a steep hill.

'Where are we going, Adonia?' panted Charlie. 'Where is the Temple of Athena?'

Adonia pointed to the giant golden building on top of the hill.

'The Parthenon', whispered Charlie.

Under the rays of the sun that seemed to get hotter as they climbed, Charlie and Adonia scuffed up a dusty dirt track. The clatter from the market faded behind them, and soon only the soft chirps from birds, with odd-looking black heads and yellow necks, could be heard. Adonia and Charlie emerged from the track, at the foot of the Parthenon. Not another person within miles.

'Wait here', said Adonia.

She left Charlie and disappeared down one side of the building.

Charlie stared at the Parthenon close up. The marble frieze glistened in the sun like a rainbow. Charlie looked at the carvings — the sculptures were perfect. More than perfect. He couldn't help but admire the building's strength and simplicity.

After a few minutes, he decided to find the section of the frieze on display in the museum — the marble slab with the warriors he had studied so often with Ted. He found the brave men on the western side of the building. Staring at the warriors, Charlie was amazed by their yellow and red clothes and their intense faces. The warriors had somehow come to life. Charlie closed his eyelids and pretended Ted was standing alongside him.

'Close your eyes Ted, you can be here. If you try hard, you can be here, right next to me.'

A light breeze drifted across his face.

Tears welled in his eyes. 'Please help me Ted. I need you. I so badly need you.'

Adonia walked around the corner and saw Charlie muttering to himself.

'Are you all right Charlie?' she asked.

No he wasn't all right. He would never be all right. He quickly turned away.

'I'm fine', he said.

Adonia gave him a strange look.

'We will enter the Temple and wait for the Oracle's final test.'

'I can do this alone, Adonia. You don't need to be here — you owe me nothing.'

'You are my friend, Charlie. I want to help you.'

'But you really don't ...'

She put her hand to Charlie's mouth and looked up. Heavy black clouds rolled across the skies like a dirty blanket.

'Come, we should go inside now — a storm is looming.'

Through giant bronze doors, carved with two lion heads, Adonia and Charlie entered the Parthenon. Charlie's sandals clicked on the marble as he zigzagged between the huge internal pillars. An eerie echo bounced off the walls. He peered through the darkness, around one of the columns, and saw a giant lady made of gold, forty feet high and staring at him with bulging eyes. Fire torches and incense sticks burned at her ankles and floodlit her massive form. A sickly herbal smell loaded his nostrils. He took a step backwards.

'It is the statue of Athena', whispered Adonia.

'I thought it was the Oracle', gasped Charlie. 'I thought she'd grown.'

Charlie coughed at the smoke coming from the incense sticks. He stared at the monstrous statue, spikes coming out of her head and snakes covering her chest.

The gold lady carried a wry smile, like she had been waiting for him.

'What do we do now?'

'We wait', said Adonia. She sat down on the marble.

Charlie pointed to the gold monster. 'Do we have to wait near her?'

Adonia shrugged.

Charlie shuffled away from Athena. But the statue's prying eyes seemed to follow him. Her constant stare unnerved him.

'Where is everyone?' he asked.

'People from the city come here on the day of worship — Sunday.'

Charlie had forgotten what day it was. He guessed it wasn't Sunday.

At the foot of the giant lady, he bent down and pulled out one of the burning torches from a sand bed. He held the torch to his face; the flames cast odd shadows in his eye sockets. He decided to have a look at the other sculptures, anything to avoid the giant lady in the middle. He saw a man screaming, with two children in his arms, coiled together by the body of a serpent. He saw a god, half man and half fish, ready to strike with his trident. He saw a large horse, front hoofs airborne, with bulging muscles and veins. But the unsettling stare of Athena persisted; her bulging eyes relentless. Charlie moved to the rear of the temple to get away from the gold lady's stare.

Along the back wall were four square plinths, like the ones in the museum. On each plinth was mounted a geometric shape, made of crystal or glass. Charlie lifted his torch in front of the first shape, a cube the size of a hat box. It was attached to the plinth by a corner, so it looked like a diamond face-on.

'What are you doing?' shouted Adonia.

'I am just looking at some crystals', replied Charlie.

Charlie moved to the next plinth and examined the four triangular faces of the pyramid. 'A tetrahedron', he whispered.

Like the cube, it was attached to the plinth by a corner. He shuffled to the third shape, an octahedron. He remembered making this shape out of cardboard in his mathematics class. He used eight equilateral triangles; four of the triangles meeting at each vertex.

Then Charlie moved to the fourth plinth. This shape had twenty triangular sides. He knew he had seen the shape before, but he couldn't remember its name. Holding the torch close up to it, the crystal sparkled like a diamond.

'The icosahedron', he said finally.

'Who are you talking to, Charlie?'

'Nobody.'

Charlie saw his reflection in the crystal. He leaned forward and with his palm gently pressed one of the triangular faces.

Suddenly, he heard a cracking sound. He jumped backwards, away from the plinth. The crystal started moving, spinning on its corner. Then the others started spinning, whipping the air into a flurry.

'Adonia, come here!' Charlie shouted. 'I touched one of these crystals and now they are all spinning.'

Adonia bounced to her feet and dashed towards Charlie. Baffled, she stared at the crystals turning on their plinths. Her nose twitched. 'Charlie — can you smell something?'

'No.'

'I smell smoke.'

Turning their heads away from the plinths, they glared at the gold lady. The giant statue was spinning as well, only spinning in a blanket of flames.

18

THE CRYSTALS

The fire smothered the statue, the goddess lost in the inferno. But then the fire separated from the statue, like a giant fireball, and started rolling around the temple, searing anything in its path.

'Quick Charlie — behind those columns!'

Adonia ran to a cluster of pillars at the front of the Temple.

Charlie sprinted after her. He popped his head around the marble and saw the fireball become airborne. It bounced from the walls to the ceiling.

'Run!' squealed Adonia. 'It is coming for us!'

'There's nowhere to go!' Charlie raced over to the front doors and shook the handles. 'They're locked!'

Adonia pointed to the corner. 'Behind the snake.'

Charlie dashed towards the serpent, and crouched with Adonia behind it.

'Look Charlie – look at Athena …'

Charlie glared at the gold lady. The spinning statue had opened its mouth.

'What is that?' His chest thumped.

Water spurted from her lips. Liquid so powerful it hit the roof and brought some timbers down. The gold lady pelted the water randomly, tumbling some of the smaller statues at the rear.

'This must be the Oracle's final test', said Adonia. 'Watch out Charlie!'

The fireball whizzed over Charlie's head. He ducked. The flames singed his hair.

Then, a wall of water slammed into Charlie's back. He toppled to the ground. The force of the liquid sent him flying across the floor on his stomach, in the direction of the four plinths with the crystals spinning on top. The liquid smacked into Adonia's legs. She too skimmed the marble tiles and crashed into a stone column.

'What is it Adonia?' shouted Charlie. 'What is the test?'

'I do not know', she cried.

Adonia crawled behind a pillar.

'Look! There is something else — growing at Athena's feet.' Charlie pointed to the gold lady.

Adonia popped her head from behind the column and caught a face full of water.

'A rock!' she spluttered. 'A mammoth rock!'

A giant boulder grew around the gold lady. And, like the flames, it separated from the statue and trundled along erratically, ready to crush anything in its path.

'Watch out Adonia — behind you!'

She dived out of the rock's path, slid across the tiles on her belly, seconds from being crushed to death. The pair huddled together behind a column, darting their eyes around the temple, trying to locate the three deadly forces.

'This test will kill us', screamed Charlie. 'Fire, water and a rock?'

'Earth … it is *Earth*.' Adonia's face lit up. 'Charlie this is about Plato's elements – these forces are Plato's *Elements!*'

Charlie ducked his head between his legs. The fireball missed his scalp by an inch.

'What elements?'

'Plato tells us there are four elements — fire, water, earth and air.'

'I can see three of them', spluttered Charlie. 'Where's the air?'

Air started to twist above the statue's head, like a cyclone, whipping up debris into its indiscriminate clutches.

Charlie glared at the gold lady. 'Spoke too soon.'

The twister crackled and expanded. Charlie's heart thumped. Within seconds, it resembled a tornado. Like the three other destroyers, it started to thrash the shrine. *Smash. Smash. Smash.* More sculptures shattered like glass. It whizzed and hissed towards Adonia.

'Put your arms around a column', yelled Charlie. 'Or you'll get sucked in!'

Adonia's hair flapped violently around her face as she gripped a column with both hands, trying to hang on to life.

Suddenly, a terrifying roar came from the gold lady's mouth, and then a voice boomed so loudly that it tumbled gold leaves from the top of the marble columns.

'Match the shapes with the elements!' bellowed the voice.

'Did you hear that, Adonia? Did you hear what the statue said?' Charlie dived out of the path of the boulder.

'Yes, I heard it!' Adonia's eyes darted away from the gold lady and in the direction of the spinning crystals.

Charlie lay on the marble as his hair blustered about his face. 'Match the shapes with the elements ... What do we do?'

'Plato teaches us that each element has a matching shape. The Oracle's final test must be to match the elements with the right crystal.'

'How are we going to do that?' shouted Charlie.

'We pull each crystal from its plinth and throw it into the eye of the right element.'

'Are you sure about this?'

'As sure as light comes from the sun.'

Adonia ducked the fireball. 'Quick Charlie — to the plinths!'

19

THE ELEMENTS

Across the rubble, Charlie dashed after Adonia. He dodged a barrage of water and watched the giant rock rumble in front of him. But he lost sight of the tornado and it caught him and hurled him to the ground. He whooshed across the tiles on his backside and thumped against the plinths. Adonia thumped next to him.

'We do the tetrahedron first', said Adonia. 'It matches the element of fire.'

Adonia and Charlie scrambled up the plinth and tugged at the crystal.

'Heave, Charlie.'

'I'm trying.'

Charlie pushed the crystal at its base with his swollen hands, the shape rotated and the edges cut into his skin. It snapped from the plinth.

'Got it!' Charlie staggered under the weight of the heavy crystal.

'Throw it into the eye of the fireball.'

'Where's the fireball?'

'Behind you!'

Charlie twisted his body. 'Arrggh!!!!!!!'

The blazing ball raged towards him. He knew he would be burned alive if Adonia's plan didn't work. He propelled the gemstone into the burning red core. *Smack*. Fireworks. The fireball dissipated into thin air.

Charlie ogled the spectacle. But there was no time to marvel.

'To the next one — the octahedron', ordered Adonia.

'Which element does that match?' Charlie slipped on the wet tiles. He struggled to stay upright.

'Plato says it matches air.'

Charlie and Adonia tugged at the shape.

'Watch out Charlie — the tornado!'

The twister ripped past Charlie. His body was almost sucked into the vacuum. Adonia grabbed Charlie's waist and he felt the strength of her arms. His tunic flapped hard and for a split second Charlie thought the twister might suck it clean off. Adonia's hair blustered into his eyes. She had saved him from being ripped apart.

They lunged at the crystal again and pulled.

'Harder!' winced Adonia.

Charlie ground his molars as he pulled.

In seconds, the octahedron snapped from the plinth. The tornado blasted straight for them. Together, they hurled the crystal into the air. The gem got sucked into the twister — and the storm dispersed in an instant.

'The icosahedron!' shouted Charlie. 'Which element?'

'It matches water!'

A wall of liquid struck Charlie's legs and toppled him. He tried to hold onto the plinth but he was catapulted five feet into the air and his shoulder blades slammed against one of the marble columns.

'I can't reach it Adonia!'

Water gushed into Charlie's face.

'Nor can I.'

Suddenly, the force of the water smashed one of the plinths into smithereens, sending the icosahedron flying into the air. Adonia dived like a jewel thief to catch the precious gem. Her cupped hands seized the crystal — in the nick of time.

'That was close ...' she whispered.

Water kept belting Charlie's body. The intensity was so strong he couldn't move his limbs. He was pinned to the column by the force of the liquid.

Adonia slid across the tiles, clutching the crystal. She clambered to her feet. Her legs trembled. She staggered, holding the shape between Charlie's face and the surging water.

'I'm going to let it go, Charlie, into the middle!'

'It will slam into my face!' gurgled Charlie.

'No — it is the only way!'

Charlie had to trust Adonia, this time with his life. She had a look in her eye, the look of a warrior. Even if he dies now, he was glad Plato had chosen her. He wouldn't want anyone else.

He watched her hands quiver like jelly. She wrestled under the weight of the twelve pointed gem. The water bombarded Charlie's face like a mortar attack. He shut his eyes, waiting for the razor-sharp gem to smack his nose. He grimaced in anticipation. Adonia eased her grip and released the spiky crystal. *Whoosh.* The water stopped gushing. Charlie couldn't believe it. He heaved a massive sigh. He was alive.

'One element left, Charlie — earth — it matches the cube!'

Crunch. Their heads turned towards the disturbing noise. The boulder had crushed the crystal cube, and the marble plinth it sat on, into smithereens.

'What do we do now?' yelled Charlie.

The boulder trundled like a giant grenade, rolling at speed, straight for them.

'Run!' screamed Adonia.

The pair sprinted to the statue of the serpent. The boulder smashed through a fluted pillar, bringing a section of the roof spiralling to the ground. The pair dodged the falling rubble and hid behind the snake. They crouched down and watched the destruction.

Charlie poked his head through the serpent's coils. The boulder gathered pace. It rattled like an avalanche towards them.

'This is it, Charlie — we can't stop it.'

Charlie knew that with the cube gone they had no hope of stopping the boulder, and death was now a certainty.

'Goodbye, my friend', whispered Adonia. 'I will see you in the next world.'

Charlie's eyes met Adonia's. She was too young to die. So was he. Anyway, he wasn't ready for death. He looked at the tiny splinters of glass from the smashed cube, and the voice from the statue rang inside his head. 'Match the shapes with the elements.' The gold lady had said to match the *shape*. Not the crystal. He needed the shape, he needed a cube. His eyes darted about the temple, looking for a cube. Then he remembered his locket.

He leapt to his feet. 'We're not going anywhere!'

Tugging at his locket, Charlie pulled the chain until it broke. Fearless, he faced the boulder head on, with the look of a fighter, the look of a warrior.

'What are you doing?' shrieked Adonia. 'Get down!'

Gripping the locket in his hands he yelled, 'It's a frigging cube!'

The boulder rolled towards Charlie as if it was purposely trying to run him down. Out of desperation, or stupidity, Charlie stood in the path of the murderous rock. He stared at the giant boulder trundling like a bulldozer, heading straight for him. Inches away from the mammoth chunk of earth, he flung the locket at the boulder, his final act of defiance. The locket smashed into the centre of the boulder's crust and the rock disintegrated into a thousand pieces.

But, then, the gold lady crumbled like a biscuit and the Oracle stepped out. She waved her rings in Charlie's direction, and a trail of light zapped him to the ground. He collapsed on the marble and lay motionless.

Adonia raced to Charlie.

'Charlie — are you all right? Are you all right?'

He didn't move. He wasn't breathing.

The Oracle glided towards Charlie's body. 'Plato tells us a god created the Physical World with the elements.'

The lion cub circled Charlie's limp body like prey.

Adonia cradled Charlie in her arms and gently stroked his face. She tried to wake him up.

'Did you know the elements came from the Eternal World? And the god put order into the elements, the geometric shapes.' Her black eyes scanned the rubble. 'But unlike the Eternal World, everything in the Physical World — this world — changes, nothing is permanent, and everything eventually decays.'

The Oracle glared at Charlie's body.

'You have killed him!' screamed Adonia. Tears started to roll down her pretty face.

'It is true he has left us', said the Oracle.

'We passed your insane tests and you killed him anyway!' cried Adonia.

Adonia picked up Charlie's broken locket from the tiles, and her sweet tears splashed on the silver box. She howled like a dying animal and rocked Charlie's head back and forth.

20

THE ETERNAL WORLD

Charlie opened his eyes. Everything was white. He was flying, soaring like a bird, migrating. Nothing he had known was with him. Nothing at all. He opened his mind and he looked for something familiar. And with his mind he could see everything. As he glided, he saw shapes made from light: a perfect square, a perfect circle, a perfect triangle. Then he saw other glowing shapes of light — forms of things. He saw a chair, and then he saw a table. Someone was seated at the table. The person stood up. Charlie heard a voice. He recognised the voice. The person walked towards him.

'Ted', whispered Charlie. 'Ted, is that you?'

'Yes, it's me, Charlie.'

Ted appeared from the whiteness, his face youthful and fresh. Not as Charlie remembered. No traces of sickness or pain.

'Where are we, Ted?' asked Charlie.

'We are in the Eternal World, Charlie.' Ted opened his arms. A feeling of warmth encased Charlie.

'Can you remember anything?' asked Ted

'I took your scroll back, Ted — just as you asked.'

'I know you did, Charlie. Thank you.'

'But then I couldn't get home. I got stuck in Ancient Greece. I couldn't find the key to get home.'

'Yes — which is the reason you are here.'

'Ted, I don't understand. I don't understand any of this.'

'Charlie, ten years ago when I first started at the museum I discovered the staircase leading to the Ancient World. I didn't understand why it was there — but I used it. Every day I went down those stairs and visited Ancient Greece. I worked in The Academy and was Plato's librarian. We became great friends. You know all those old scrolls I used to show you Charlie — they were all from The Academy's library.'

Charlie looked confused. 'So you worked two jobs.'

'Yes, I did.' Ted grinned as if he was pleased with himself. 'Two jobs. And, Charlie, over time, I came to appreciate Plato's ideas in full. He is truly an extraordinary man. I realised that Plato's ideas were not that different from my beliefs. He believes in a god, life after death, and an Eternal World. It occurred to me that the staircase in the library had something to do with his ideas. It belonged to the Eternal World where time doesn't exist. That's why I could travel through time.'

Charlie smiled at Ted as he spoke. He was so happy to see him again. His heart swelled with joy.

'I think Plato knew the staircase was special. He knew it led to different times. But he never used it himself. And although I never asked Plato directly, I am sure he knew I was from a different time and a different place', said Ted. His face looked thoughtful.

'But, Charlie, a month ago, when I was working in The Academy's library, the Oracle came in. She said she was visiting Plato, but it was as though she was seeking me out. And, Charlie, I had heard about the Oracle. I knew she was a divine being who knew everything.'

'You have met the Oracle?' asked Charlie.

'Oh, yes', said Ted. 'She is quite something — isn't she? And that cub of hers — vicious little creature.'

Charlie clenched his teeth. 'Vicious all right.'

'The Oracle told me to leave the library at once. I asked her why I needed to go immediately. She said I would die soon; my time on earth was drawing to a close. I should be with people from my time, my family, when I passed away. So I tidied up my desk and left. But, Charlie, as I went through the library door she said the strangest of things.'

'What did she say?'

'She said your name, Charlie.'

'But why?'

'I had no idea. So I asked her. Why did you say Charlie? I said. She told me that my grandson, called Charlie, would never recover from my death.'

'She told you that?' said Charlie.

'She told me you couldn't see the Eternal World — you couldn't see a heaven. As you could imagine, Charlie, I was shocked to hear this. It troubled me.'

Charlie felt guilty, as though he had caused Ted pain.

'So I asked her if there was anything I could do. She took a scroll off one of the shelves and gave it to me. Tell Charlie to return it, she said. Then she took the key out of the door and held it up to the light. She asked me if I knew that the key was Eternal. I didn't know that, Charlie — it just looked like an old key. She said that when Charlie arrives in the library to return the scroll, the door would be locked and you wouldn't be able to get back.'

Ted seemed concerned.

'I didn't like the sound of that, Charlie; I thought it would scare you. Being in Ancient Greece all by yourself — not able to get back.'

But then Ted smiled. 'You know what, Charlie, the Oracle told me not to worry. After my death, she would see to it that the key was delivered to me in the Eternal World. She told me you would come looking for it. You would come to the Eternal World and see it for yourself. And so, Charlie, here you are.'

Charlie stared at Ted. He suddenly realised that he hadn't returned the scroll for Ted. He had returned it for himself so he could see the Eternal World — a world he couldn't see with his mind.

Ted lifted his hand and opened his palm; a key glowed with the purest of light. He passed the key to Charlie. Although Charlie wasn't lifting his arm, he felt his limb rise. A warm object had become wrapped in his fingers.

'So this whole journey has been for me?' Charlie whispered.

Tears started to well in his eyes.

'Yes Charlie. This is your sign. And as you can see — I am more than all right.'

Ted glowed like an angel. A strange warmth enveloped Charlie's heart.

'But Ted ... Why did we have to do all those crazy tests from the Oracle?'

Ted smiled lovingly at his grandson.

'Charlie, the Oracle is a friend of Plato's and a great believer in his ideas. In her own way, she was leading you here — to the Eternal World. Every one of her tests, every one of Plato's ideas — the story of the cave, the ideal city, the elements — they all lead to Plato's biggest idea — the existence of the Eternal World.'

'So she was on our side all along?'

'Yes, she was.'

Tears streamed down Charlie's cheeks.

'And so, Charlie, Plato's ideas are just another way of looking at things. But you didn't need a sign. You didn't need a message. And you didn't need to do the Oracle's tests. The answers to your questions were inside you all along. The light of your mind, Charlie — it's called faith.'

Ted's hand gently touched Charlie's face and the tears fell away.

'Nice seeing you again, Charlie.'

Charlie's body felt tranquil, like he was floating.

Then a serious look fell across Ted's face. 'But Charlie, before you go back home, I have one more favour to ask of you.'

'What Ted, what is it?'

'Plato is very ill, Charlie.'

'I saw Plato at The Academy', said Charlie. 'I think he is going to die.'

'Yes', said Ted. 'He will die if nothing is done. Plato is a young man and in his short life he has done much but on paper he has written only one book — *The Apology* — which is the scroll you returned. But if he lives longer he will write many more, and people for centuries to come will marvel at his thinking.'

Ted seemed reflective.

'So, Charlie, I had to do something about Plato's illness. I couldn't stand by and let him die. I knew our modern medicines could save him. So I got my hands on some penicillin and rolled it up in the scroll you returned. If Plato takes the medicine in time, he will recover.'

Charlie glared at Ted, horrified. 'But, Ted, I didn't take the scroll out of the container. I didn't know there was medicine in it. I put the scroll in the library — back on the shelf.'

'Don't worry, Charlie', Ted raised his hands to calm Charlie down. 'I knew you would be coming here to the Eternal World and I could tell you myself about the medicine. You need to return to The Academy, find the scroll, and get the medicine to Plato. You need to do this before you go home. You don't belong here in the Eternal World — not yet — not for a long time. And you don't belong in Ancient Greece. You belong home with your mum and dad — they need you to take care of them.'

Ted raised his arms, gave Charlie the warmest of hugs and smiled.

'Goodbye, Charlie — I will see you later — much later.'

'But Ted wait …' said Charlie.

Charlie felt his head rocking back and forth.

He heard a cry. 'Wake up, Charlie … wake up!'

Batting his eyelids open, he saw Adonia's panicked eyes staring straight at him. He felt something in his hand. He opened his palm and saw a key radiating pure light, like a star.

21

THE HORSE

'I thought you were dead', Adonia cried.

'Indeed he was', said the Oracle. The lion cub nibbled at Charlie's ear.

'I have the key, Adonia.' The key sparkled between Charlie's fingers. 'We have to get back to The Academy — we can save Plato.'

'Plato is leaving this world soon', said the Oracle. 'I fear you will be too late.'

'He can't die', snapped Charlie. 'He has only written one book.'

'The Academy is two hours by foot from here', said Adonia. She glared at the Oracle. 'You can help us. We need a horse.'

'Help ... help.' She waved her hands in the air. Her rings rolled around her fingers. 'Everyone seeks nothing but help from the Oracle. So tiresome it becomes.'

She yawned.

'But you like Plato', shouted Charlie. 'You are a friend of his. You visited him at The Academy — why won't you help us save him?'

'My dear boy, have you not learned anything? It is neither here nor there what happens to Plato, either way he lives.'

'But he has big ideas that need to be written down — ideas to be appreciated for generations to come. What about that?' Charlie yelled.

'It is true, Plato is a literary genius.' The Oracle looked at the cub. 'Very well, I will help you.'

'Spiros', she said. The cat flashed its pointy fangs.

'Into the finest horse.'

The cub disappeared under the rubble. Charlie's eyes scanned the room. Where had the nasty little creature gone? He clambered to his feet, dusted his robe and scanned the temple, trying to locate the cat.

Suddenly, Charlie heard a crumbling noise behind him. As he turned, he felt the ground underneath his sandals tremor. He saw a horse — the statue had come alive. The huge animal trotted towards him. Reins swung from a long neck and muscles burst through the short white hair of its powerful legs. But then Charlie saw the glassy eyes of the animal — black diamonds.

Within seconds, Adonia had grabbed the straps and mounted the creature. She looked formidable on the stallion, like a warrior preparing for battle.

'Jump on, Charlie, behind me.' She held out her hand.

Spiros jolted sideways and flared his wet nostrils.

Sweat trickled down Charlie's forehead. He had never been on a horse before. Terrified, he grabbed Adonia's strong hand. She nearly crushed his fingers. As he leapt, a gust of air swept beneath him, and Charlie landed on the animal's back. He gripped Adonia at the waist.

'Faster than the bow of Apollo', yelled the Oracle.

Adonia kicked Spiros with her heels. 'To The Academy!'

The bronze doors flung open and Spiros galloped out of the Temple. His ears pricked high and his tail swished. The Oracle waved to her pet as it disappeared into the night, her rings glistening under the stars. With a glance Charlie looked back, to view the Parthenon for the last time. He saw the Oracle step into the crumbling statue of Athena. She fluttered her fingers and restored the destruction in seconds. The Temple was back to its glory days, glistening white and gold. He smiled and wondered where the Oracle was now, in his time. The Parthenon desperately needed her.

As Spiros galloped through the mist, Charlie bobbed up and down like a floating cork. Adonia's long hair flicked him in the face. He kept on thinking about what Ted had said about Plato. If he lives a long life he will write many books, and people for centuries to come will marvel at his thinking. He needed to save Plato. He couldn't let Ted down now.

✳ ✳ ✳

In the early hours of the morning, Adonia and Charlie dismounted Spiros in The Academy's courtyard. They sprinted into the library. Xenophon sat at her desk and

120

dutifully stitched pouches under the dim light of an oil lamp. Dedicated to her craft, the safekeeping of the scrolls was more important than her eyesight.

'Xenophon, *The Apology*', panted Charlie. 'Where is it?'

Her eye moved from the pouch to Charlie.

'Why good sir, *The Apology* is out — it has been borrowed.'

'Borrowed ... borrowed by whom?'

Xenophon slowly put down her tools and toddled to one of the shelves. Her wrinkled hands picked up a scroll.

'Good sir, I will have to check the records.'

She took some time to unravel it; the scroll was a table length long.

Charlie tapped his sandals on the tiles. 'Can you look it up quickly?'

Somehow, Xenophon sensed the urgency, and her eye moved faster down the scroll.

'Glaucon', she said. 'Good sir, Glaucon has borrowed it.'

'Where is he?' snapped Adonia.

'I believe he is with his brother, Plato.'

Adonia and Charlie raced through The Academy's main building. Their clicking heels echoed around the giant rooms. When they reached Plato's room, they didn't bother knocking. They flung open the door and charged in. Glaucon sat at Plato's bedside and strummed his lyre softly; his eyes glued to the tiles. When he heard their footsteps, he lifted his heavy head, and his voice quivered with grief.

'Only a minute ago Plato left us', he whispered. 'His soul has migrated to the Eternal World.'

22

THE ETERNAL KEY

Charlie saw a pouch on Plato's bedside table. *The Apology* was stitched into the side. He raced to the table, knocked the fruit and the cake flying in his panic and snatched up the leather cylinder. Furiously, he tugged at the strings and opened the lid, splitting the leather down the side. He tipped the cylinder on its head and a scroll dropped into his hands.

'What are you doing?' cried Glaucon.

Charlie ignored Glaucon. Quickly, he unravelled the scroll and found a plastic tube filled with clear liquid in the centre.

Glaucon's eyes widened.

'We need to sit him up', said Charlie. 'Adonia, help me.'

Charlie and Adonia heaved Plato upright, and Glaucon propped cushions behind his brother's back.

Charlie could feel that Plato's body was limp, but still warm. He popped the plastic cap off the tube and sniffed the medicine. A horrible medical smell wafted into the air. Whatever Ted had put into the tube, it was potent. Charlie tilted Plato's head backwards and dribbled a small amount of the fluid in between Plato's grey lips, spilling some of the mixture down his chin.

Then, under his tunic, Charlie pulled out the eternal key. He thought that if the key belonged to the Eternal World, it might have eternal powers. He placed the key on Plato's heart. They all stared at Plato, motionless, anxious for a response. They waited and waited for the medicine to take effect. But Plato's body didn't move.

Then, Glaucon lifted his lyre from his lap.

'I ask only one thing of you, Charlie', said Glaucon. He placed the instrument into Charlie's hands. 'Do me, and my brother's soul, the greatest of honours — please play.'

Charlie took the heavy instrument from Glaucon's hands. He remembered his guitar at home — the guitar he hadn't touched since Ted's death. The lyre trembled in his hands. He slowly started to strum. He played the minors. He played the majors. He played with all of his heart. The soft notes hung in the air like a veil of harmonies.

From the courtyard, Spiros poked his long white nose through the window. The horse's glassy eyes stared at the limp body, hopeful to see Plato's body return to the living. And for a second there, Charlie thought he saw a reflection of the Oracle in the animal's eyes. He strummed and he strummed.

Then, the warmth from the Eternal World came. Plato's eyes fluttered. Charlie played the lyre louder. Adonia poured more medicine between Plato's lips and he started to sip small amounts of the fluid. Tears streamed down Glaucon's cheeks. He leaned across the bed and held his younger brother in his arms like he would never let him go.

Plato's eyes opened slowly and focused on Charlie. The look Plato gave Charlie was strange, but peaceful. As if Plato wasn't looking for something inside Charlie anymore.

Charlie stopped strumming.

'Like your spirit, Charlie, your melody is beautiful', whispered Plato. 'Rhythm and harmony always find their way to the inward places of the soul.'

Slowly, Plato lifted the key from his chest. He stretched across Glaucon and placed the eternal key in Charlie's hand. The key shone like the sun.

'Take the key, Charlie, take it with you. It is not needed here in Greece. And take with you the light of your mind.'

Charlie began to strum again. He played the harmony of Plato. He played the harmony of Ted. He played the harmonies of angels. The tunes from the Eternal World lifted his heart.

23

THE FAREWELL

Charlie and Adonia stood in front of the door in the library. Fighting hard to keep the tears away, Charlie knew he would not be coming back. He would never see Adonia's pretty face again. In a weird way, saying goodbye to Adonia was like saying goodbye to Ted, only worse.

'Thank you.' Charlie fidgeted with the rope around his tunic. 'For everything you have done for me.'

'I forgot to return your locket', said Adonia. She reached under her tunic and pulled out the little silver box. 'I found it on the floor of the Temple.'

She held out the locket, the broken chain dangling.

'Keep it', said Charlie. He folded her hands over the silver box. 'I don't need it anymore.'

'Are you sure?'

'Positive.'

Adonia tied the broken chain behind her neck, under her long hair. The silver box sparkled against her tanned skin. She leaned forward and kissed Charlie gently.

Charlie held her, and held on to the moment. A single tear drifted aimlessly down his face. His heart ached. Although he wanted to, he couldn't hold her forever. He had to let her go. Release her back to her warrior life and her warrior thoughts. She belonged in The Academy. She belonged in Ancient Greece. He sucked in his emotions and stepped back.

'You are a great warrior, Adonia.'

'As are you, my friend.'

Charlie pulled out the eternal key from under his tunic and carefully placed it into the lock. He glanced at the new head librarian.

'*The Apology*, Xenophon, the pouch will need some repairs. I am sorry.'

Xenophon's eye looked up from her stitching.

'Every pouch can be repaired, good sir. May your journey home be a safe one.' A warm smile crossed Xenophon's face.

The winged lady statue hovered above, her sword skyward in a victory salute.

Charlie heard the door click, without the key being turned. He had never seen a lock like it. Part of him wanted to stay and study it. But then again, it was an eternal key so it probably was an eternal lock. He pulled the key out and held it tightly in his hand. He turned to face Adonia one last time.

'Go Charlie', she said. 'Return to the world you came from.'

She waved him on. She was a girl of action, not of words.

Charlie smiled at her and slowly walked through the door, holding the eternal key. He heard the door close gently behind him. He missed Adonia already. But the key spread light over the darkness in his heart. He felt the warmth of the key in his hand. He stood at the foot of the staircase and took a deep breath. Then the key started glowing, brighter and brighter. It illuminated everything around him. He could see everything.

Walking up the stairs, Charlie moved slowly at first. But after a while, he couldn't feel the steps on his heels — it was as though he was climbing through air. In a flash, his body shot upwards like a rocket. His stomach dropped to his toes. He soared like a bird; flying higher than any bird from earth, higher than he had ever been. The heaviness from his linen tunic lifted. The pain from the sunburn, the bruises and the cuts all disappeared. Wind drifted across his face as he floated in light and warmth. He stretched out his arms and closed his eyes. He was migrating.

Thump. Charlie crash-landed. He lay face down on a cold concrete floor at the top of a staircase. He scrambled to his feet and saw a familiar door. He pushed it open. He stepped into Ted's research room. The soft glow from the desk lamp lit up the room. He wiggled his feet in his black school shoes, brushed down the creases of his grey trousers and flicked his school tie over his shoulder. He put the eternal key in his pocket and glanced at his watch — 11.15 a.m. Time hadn't changed.

Then he remembered something Ted had said. The staircase had something to do with Plato's ideas. It belonged to the Eternal World where time didn't exist. *That's why time hadn't moved forward*, thought Charlie. *It didn't exist.*

He grinned as he strained his ears, listening for the security guard. Sounds of footsteps didn't come. He scurried into the corridors of the basement and headed for the stairwell.

24

THE ANSWER

Charlie caught up with his class in the portrait gallery. He shuffled towards the back of the group with his hands in his pockets, trying to look inconspicuous. It worked. Nobody blinked an eyelid. He looked for Mr Hollingbury who stood amongst a group of statues, flapping his notepad in the air.

'Now, class, this man over here', he pointed, 'his name is Plato. Has anyone ever heard of Plato?'

Silence from the class.

Charlie stared at the face of the statue.

'He was a philosopher who lived more than 2000 years ago, in Ancient Greece. He had some remarkable ideas, which are still being talked about today. Can you imagine that — your ideas being talked about 2000 years on.'

Mr Hollingbury grinned at the class.

'Plato lived a long life; he died in his eighties and wrote more than twenty books.'

A wry smile crossed Charlie's face.

Herding the class like sheep, Mr Hollingbury hurried the students to the next exhibit. Charlie stayed behind to study the statue of Plato. He stared at the eyes of the man he had met. Carefully, with his fingers, he reached forward and touched the statue's cold cheek bones. Then in his pocket, he felt the eternal key radiate warmth. He reached for the key but he felt someone grab his hand. He couldn't see anyone standing next to him, but he could feel a presence. He heard breathing. It was Ted.

Charlie and Ted stood there, hand in hand, studying the Plato exhibit. Just like the old days. It was as if nothing had changed. Charlie felt Ted's happiness. And he looked forward to the day he would see Ted again, in the Eternal World. After a few minutes Charlie felt the warmth in his hand slowly leave him.

'Goodbye Ted', he whispered

But the warmth in Charlie's heart stayed. It never left him. He smiled, contented, and stood alone for a minute, lost in his thoughts. He left the Plato statue and walked slowly to the next exhibit. He mingled with his friends and watched Mr Hollingbury hover around a glass box. In it was the strangest of instruments.

'Now does anyone know what this is?' asked the teacher.

Nobody bothered with an answer.

'Anyone', snapped Mr Hollingbury. He pushed out his lower lip.

Charlie raised his hand.

'Yes, Charlie.' The teacher seemed grateful for a response.

'It's a lyre.'

'Very good, Charlie.' Mr Hollingbury's face glowed. 'Very good indeed.'

ABOUT THE AUTHOR

Ali Gray lives in Sydney, Australia with her husband and their two daughters. *Plato's Academy and the Eternal Key* is Ali's first novel. To find out more about Ali, visit www.aligray.com.au

CPSIA information can be obtained at www.ICGtesting.com
Printed in the USA
LVOW12s1453030415

433203LV00001B/19/P